TRUST
in Action

TRUST
in Action

A Leader's Guide to
Act. Right. Now.

Jim Massey

Route 2
Chevy Chase, MD

Copyright © 2023 by Jim Massey
www.jimmassey.co

All rights reserved. No part of this book may be reproduced or used in any manner without written permission of the copyright owner except for the use of quotations in a book review.

First paperback edition 2023

Cover and book design by Sheila Parr

Hardcover ISBN: 979-8-9876976-0-3
Paperback ISBN: 979-8-9876976-1-0
Ebook ISBN: 979-8-9876976-2-7

Published by Route 2, LLC
www.jimmassey.co

Dedication

Humanity. We are the cause; we can be the change.

Earth. We are trying to cut through the B.S. and save you.

You (yes, you). Trust yourself. It's time to act right now. Be and do good.

The way to make people trustworthy is to trust them.

—**Ernest Hemingway**

TRUST
in Action

Contents

Acknowledgments xiii

Foreword xv

Introduction 1

    Chapter 1: Collecting the Dots 11

    Chapter 2: In Business We Trust 23

    Chapter 3: Can, Care, Do. 33

Part 1: Can 45

    Chapter 4: Why Do You Exist? 47

    Chapter 5: The Purpose of Purpose 57

    Chapter 6: The Value of Values 65

Part 2: Care 75

    Chapter 7: Show Me More 77

    Chapter 8: Humanity at Work 87

    Chapter 9: What on Earth? 97

Part 3: Do 105

    Chapter 10: Stepping Into the B.S. 107

    Chapter 11: This I Know 113

    Chapter 12: Act Right Now. 121

    Chapter 13: Ready. Set. Go!. 133

About the Author 137

Acknowledgments

In December of 2019, I decided to take a buy-out from a job I loved. I knew it was time to find my next challenge. Fast forward to a few months after my decision and the world was completely changed. We were thrown into a global lockdown due to COVID-19 and everything we thought we knew about work would change.

Personally, I was shocked by how much of my identity was tied to work. It was one of the biggest, unforeseen challenges I've faced to date, and with this realization, I knew that I wanted to write a book.

Now that I've accomplished this dream, I want to wholeheartedly say thank you to all the people who encouraged me during this time and built the emotional infrastructure I needed to trust myself and bring *Trust in Action* to fruition.

First, my family: Emily, my wife, and my two sons Sawyer

and Lawson. We have conquered the fifty United States and seven continents together and still found time to write *GeoKids: 50 States on School Breaks*, all while pursuing our life's work. Thank you for the support, humor, and the honest feedback throughout the process.

I also want to thank my mom and dad. Thank you for teaching me early that my ideas matter, that I have a voice I must use, and that I can do whatever I set my mind to.

Thank you to my #MizzouMade friends; you've been here through thick and thin! Also, I want to acknowledge the important mentorship I've received along the way from Angela Barfield, Alison Taylor, Mark Perera, Matt Hill, Jennifer Brown, Dame Polly Courtice, and Susan Angele. You inspire me to keep fighting.

This book could not have come to life without the expertise of my book team. I want to give a special thanks to Tina Chang the founder of Pioneering Collective for her tireless support. Thank you also to Scott James, my publishing guide, for keeping me on task, Kyoko Minegishi, marketing guru, for helping me find my brand and build www.jimmassey.co, Daron Christopher, executive communications expert, for helping me stay concisely on point, Sheila Parr, my book designer, for the stunning cover, and Rae Freudenberger for editing the manuscript. Your skill, knowledge, support, and brilliance shocks me every day. Thank you for believing in what we can do together.

Ken Sterling at Big Speak—extraordinaire, and oh captain, my captain—thank you for bringing me along.

Finally, thank you to Shannon Constantine Logan for helping me get pen to paper and find the words to drive change for good.

Foreword

For many years, I had the honor of serving as a founding member of AstraZeneca's Sustainability Advisory Board. I saw firsthand the company's focus on the bold goal of transforming into one of the world's most sustainable companies.

In 2016, I met the company's new Global Vice President of Sustainability, Jim Massey. In addition to being responsible for the advisory board, he was also tasked with bringing all key sustainability programs into one global team. In essence, this meant Jim would be responsible for all environmental programs, access to healthcare strategy, and the enterprise ethics and transparency initiatives. No small task.

I first learned about Jim's background during our initial interaction over a conference call. Jim had just overhauled the global compliance team and had many years of experience in governance. However, he had limited to no experience in environment matters and, though he had commercial experience, he had not worked in public health or access to health care outside the United States.

Over the course of building the new sustainability program, *Lead with Health*, Jim regularly consulted me on the program, its progress, as well as future topics on which he should focus. As his advisor, I always looked forward to his updates. He was a rarity in the boardroom—a true creative thinker who intuitively understood the need for holistic thinking to solve the complex problems facing the company and its stakeholders, especially the people who relied on the company's products. Jim understood that we needed to embrace new ways of working to meet new challenges and that we needed to form effective partnerships in order to drive innovation.

One of the most novel programs I have seen from a global pharmaceutical company was a result of the work of Jim's team and research colleagues at the Cambridge Institute for Sustainability Leadership, where I was the founding Director and led the team for three decades.

The partnership sought to research what happened when a low-income community in western Kenya was equipped with a clean, green alternative cooking fuel—biogas—and monitor how the resulting 'fuel shift' was perceived, trialed, and ultimately embraced by its households. The end goal for the AstraZeneca sustainability team was to further understand how changing human behavior could change the course of respiratory disease by preventing the cause of the disease itself.

I saw Jim's leadership approach in action—always inspiring his teams to go further, try a different option, or find a new partnership to scale their impact. As Jim progressed the 'Lead with Health' program, he consistently demonstrated his willingness to learn, tackle new projects, and make a positive impact. I came to see that a key to his success was showing genuine empathy for those with whom he interacts.

Above all, Jim's most distinguishing characteristic is his ability to deliver on what he committed. He walks his talk. I am excited he has used these leadership characteristics to help define the trust model he shares in *Trust in Action: The Leader's Guide to Act Right Now*.

Jim truly lives by his trust in action model. It was rewarding to help guide him through challenges, see his progress, and finally, to encourage his momentum. Ultimately, I watched Jim grow into a leader who was not just capable of driving environmental and social programs, but leading one of the world's first seven Net Zero pledges at AstraZeneca by fostering trust and taking robust action at every step.

As a long-time leader in the sustainability space—and someone growing increasingly impatient with inaction as we approach irreversible environmental change—I understand the importance of action. Now more than ever, we must trust each other and work collectively and creatively to address the problems we face today.

For leaders reading this—no matter where you are or the work you do or the job title that you hold—you have a role to play. Jim's book contains valuable lessons on learning to trust yourself and take action, and I am confident you will benefit greatly from these pages.

—**Dame Polly Courtice, DBE, LVO, DL**
  Emeritus Director and Senior Ambassador, University of Cambridge Institute for Sustainability Leadership

Introduction

It was 2019. I was on a flight back from Indonesia where I had seen firsthand the broken healthcare system: lack of healthcare infrastructure, scarce medical equipment, and no public health policy to help protect and serve the people were just a few of the issues facing the country. To give you an idea of the scale of the concerns, there is an estimated one hospital bed per 1,000 people and only 25 doctors per 100,000 people. That's less than half the standard ratio of 2.4 beds per 1,000 people in the U.S. It is not uncommon for a patient to travel hours to get to a hospital only to find that the facility doesn't have the basic equipment or the appropriately trained healthcare worker to help treat what is ailing the patient. While I was there, I also learned a depressing statistic: 40 percent of Indonesian boys 13–15 years old smoke, the fastest growing smoking population in the world. As I tried to relax on my flight, the knowledge of this weighed heavily on my heart.

I was also missing both of my sons' baseball games, and I had working parent guilt. My wife would be attending, so at least one parent was there, but I was regretting not being there to watch them play. I thought, "What is more important—my work-life balance or my life's work?"

Then it hit me: my kids were safe and on their way to their baseball games. The young men in Indonesia who were already in the workforce—the boys who were my sons' ages, 10 to 13, who could buy cigarettes more easily than they could obtain clean drinking water—were not.

It wasn't about work-life: I needed to worry about my *life's* work. I have always had a passion for the human side of my work. This was the pivotal moment and the catalyst I needed to get out of this self-absorbed mindset and into one more aligned with my sense of purpose.

And there was no time to lose because we were entering the decade of our lives.

Going into 2020, those of us in the industry who were trying to be catalysts for good in both impact and permanence knew we had to start doing better, more, and faster. This was the decade where we were either going to solve problems or the climate would change so much that our window for solutions would close forever. Time matters. Every five weeks, we lose one percent of the decade.

In 2015, Sustainable Development Goals were laid out by the U.N. as a call-to-action for people worldwide to address five critical areas of importance by 2030: people, planet, prosperity, peace, and partnership. As we entered the fourth quarter of 2020, it was clear that none of the 169 metrics were on track to be met, and the U.N. made its official statement. Wildfires, water crises, and droughts were only the canaries in the proverbial coal mine. It is estimated that by August of 2022 we will already have warmed the planet -1 degrees Celsius (the event the Paris Agreement was trying to halt). As we entered the "decade of our lives," the truth was that I wasn't seeing companies transition quickly enough from saying "we will do good" to actually *doing good*. The pressure on me to do something about it only grew.

Traveling the world as the Global Vice President of Sustainability for AstraZeneca, I saw the growing issues we were facing firsthand. I'll never forget on June 20th, 2019, waking up to headlines like, "What Would You Do Without Water?" It was more than just a crisis somewhere far from home. They were addressing the situation in Chennai, India where more than 2,500 of my AstraZeneca colleagues worked with countless friends and family in the community.

I immediately started emailing other leaders to find out what we were doing to address the crisis. Within minutes, I learned the company already had plans in place to ensure employees had access to safe drinking water. Fantastic.

End of story? Not even the beginning. Local employees and leaders knew there was more we could and must do.

On August 23, armed with a desire to impact change for good, AstraZeneca Chennai employees, under the guidance of the local leadership team members and in partnership with the Environmentalist Foundation of India, decided to bring about change in spades. Before machines were brought in to restore their local water source, work began by hand, carefully picking up and digging out plastic waste from the pond. My colleagues gathered on the banks of the Nattar Street Pond in Chennai. Bright blue gloves were handed over, masks were donned, and with purposeful strides, this group set about picking up plastic and other waste. Rakes were distributed to sift beneath the layers of waste and find rubbish that had been building up for years.

One step at a time towards sustainability.

Restoring lakes and ponds will make Chennai resilient to climate change, recharge the groundwater, and ensure the flora and fauna of the city are given space to flourish.

Even though this was an important lesson, I realized other global business leaders, like me, weren't solving this problem or any other problems holistically; we were looking for fast, simple solutions, like just shipping water. At the end of the day, it was individual local business leaders who had to lead the initiative that made the most difference for that community. This is a perfect example of the transition companies need to make. Global commitments are great, but local action makes the difference. Companies are so focused on proving they are capable of change by making big pledges decades out, that they are not taking action on pilot programs, failing fast, and improving in real time. This is the type of culture that bigger companies try to espouse, but, because of bureaucracy, they struggle to deliver. The issue is that we are well beyond the time for "trying."

Companies had proven they were capable of change, but they still appeared not to care because no one was acting. Time and time again, organizations would make sweeping commitments and never demonstrate they were fulfilling them. And I wasn't the only one to notice.

Researchers looked at why companies aren't delivering on their climate commitments. They concluded the problem was lack of alignment, both with external stakeholders and within the leadership team. Fifty-eight percent of executives in one study said there were "significant differences of opinion within the leadership team" on balancing short-term priorities with long-term goals.

As environmental, social, and governance topics became more relevant and the pressure kept mounting, I had more and more leaders coming to me saying, "I don't know what to do" or "we don't know where to begin." In some cases, these were Fortune 50 leaders, the people directly in charge of governance for their companies. If business leaders knew they needed to act and were willing to act, but they weren't able to do so, I wondered what was holding companies back.

My conclusion was that it comes down to trust. In my experience, trust (or lack thereof, rather) was underpinning the polarization and misalignment of priorities we were experiencing in countries as well as in companies. We see companies breaking trust with customers all the time via viral videos (United flight attendants dragging a passenger off a plane), and employees are taking to social media to call out companies that don't fulfill their promises (Facebook/Meta having research that described societal harm its platform was causing and neglecting to act). Without knowing it, businesses erode trust with their stakeholders, and yet they are still the most trusted institutions to date.

According to Pew research, right now we have near record low levels of trust in government (19 percent) and media (34 percent), and the highest trust in business at 61 percent. What's even more interesting for me is that the majority of employees, 77 percent, says that they trust their employer. As a company, gaining the trust of your employees is paramount. Trust must be seen and felt. Trust in action is all about the perseverance we face as we interact with the norms and rules surrounding how we should act and think.

In a world where society is rapidly losing trust in our systems, businesses still have some degree of trust. Business leaders must provide clarity over certainty and show the world how to Act. Right. Now. Companies are going to have to step up and lead the way. Climate change, racial tensions, gender inequities, and polarized societies have been present for a while, and COVID -19 revealed our broken global systems like government, health, financial, housing, and food. As the systems continue to divide, each of us has a role to play in changing our current trajectory. It all begins with our ability to build trust, the foundation for getting things done. Trust proves we are capable, have others interests at heart, and will do what we say.

Trust is foundational.

Since the mid 2000s, I had been working on a quick and easy way to evaluate trust: a trust model. This model would help me quickly and effectively evaluate any relationship and see what I can do to change it for the better. As I worked with my team and leaders across industries, I realized I was providing a much-needed missing piece. Colleagues were able to use my approach to help change the direction of action, and I realized it was paramount that I inspire as many leaders into action as possible. Using an updated version of this trust model and a unique take on the Self → Team → System change dynamic, this book contains a breakthrough framework for sparking action rooted in trust. After all, trust is the foundation of action. If leaders can learn to begin trusting themselves, and then to work with their teams to address and solve a problem, real action becomes possible.

Many of the topics I cover in this book are considered areas of environmental, social, and governance, or ESG, a framework that is increasingly polarizing itself. As companies, we don't have the luxury of inaction. We have customers, communities, employees, and shareholders who rely on us to keep things moving. As a society, we are more aligned than not on the biggest challenges we face. It is up to us to operate regardless of what the far ends of the political spectrum may think. This book can be used as a toolset to transcend politics and polarization and allow companies to operate with trust, which is a common denominator for all people. The information in these chapters should help you understand what actions businesses can take, what is required, and how to take responsibility in a way that inspires leaders to action and ultimately drives positive change.

Maybe you opened this book because you're a business leader who is just beginning your ESG journey and you want to learn more, or you might be a leader in a Fortune 500 who knows they need to start the work but doesn't know where to begin. You might be the founder of a unicorn startup who is ready for a new model of business. Or you might just be someone who cares about ESG and fairness in the workplace, but doesn't know how you fit in the grand scheme of things. This book will provide you with clarity on how to move forward and drive change in the direction you want.

Admitting we don't know is tough. The material in these chapters is designed to move you past the fear, the paralysis, the self-doubt, and the imposter syndrome that everyone experiences. As a leader, you will learn to trust yourself in a way that allows you to rise above the "white noise" at the system level and to take action in areas where you will have the greatest impact. My goal is to inspire you to step into the trust model, get rooted in why it matters, understand how others have achieved their success, and tap into the motivation to figure out your own version of "what comes next."

This book will be your resource to deal with various challenging business topics. Ideally, by the time you are done reading it, you will understand how you can transform yourself to transform your teams to transform the world. Consider it your "Business Leaders Cliff Notes on Trust."

At the turn of the decade, as we began to realize that countries could not meet the demands of our changing climate fast enough, everyone started asking who can? The answer: businesses. The truth is that businesses can adapt faster than governments, especially as we see governments looking inward and less globally. However, business can only do so much. The question remains, "Who is responsible?" The answer is simple.

I am responsible.

You are responsible. Each of us, as an individual, as part

of various teams, and as people who share one planet—*we* are responsible. And it's time for each of us to lead and Act. Right. Now.

Stay in the fight, not the flight, by learning to build trust.

Let's do this.

1
Collecting *the* Dots

Most people are linear thinkers. They are data driven; they thrive on structure, rules, formulas, and patterns. They have a starting point and ending point and one path to get to the goal. As a result, companies base their development programs on this model of thinking—and, oftentimes, being a linear thinker is synonymous with success. Likewise, most leaders are easily recognized by these traits because that's who we're trained to notice in society.

My whole life, people always told me that I was different, but I never quite understood how. After a particularly memorable incident in Sunday school where I would not stop challenging the church's authority, my parents simply said, "Jim, you see the world differently."

As a non-linear thinker, I tend to solve problems by taking multiple routes and piecing together the best parts, regardless of the path. I often find multiple solutions to one problem and help teams find a solution that works on multiple levels. Even though this is my normal way of thinking, I eventually learned to adapt to linear thinking as this is the default setting in so many of the corporate cultures in which I worked.

One time, about mid-career, the company I was working for had me complete a leadership assessment index as part of a leadership development program. When the test results came back, I got a call from one of the coaches. She told me my test was one of the most extreme examples they had ever seen of a non-linear thinker. The facilitators asked her to speak to me because they agreed that the leadership program as designed wouldn't be the best program for my preferences and abilities. Anxiously, I asked, "Is that normal?"

I was sitting at the desk in my hotel room in Chicago looking out the window at Lake Michigan, and I remember tears rolling down my face as she gave me her answer. She said, "You are beautifully normal, but you're not contextually normal for what companies want."

It was the first time someone actually saw me as the real me.

My whole life I had felt like an imposter, but I also walked through life effortlessly. By nature of who I was by birth—a Western, white, male (I'm even right handed)—I was accepted everywhere I went, and yet I never quite fit in. I can remember times during my education when I was told to stop asking questions and just focus on learning. I became conditioned to do this and do it exceptionally well. In fact, I was the salutatorian of my class and graduated college with no debt thanks to academic and leadership scholarships. But it never felt natural to me; I always felt like I was hiding myself.

According to this coach, between the ages of 12 and 14-years-old, we start wearing the mask society wants to see. By the time we are middle aged, as we start to appreciate life and feel a sense of mortality, we begin to question—*is this the mask for me?* That's where midlife crises come into play. People think you're acting differently, yet what is really happening is that you are showing up as yourself for the first time.

I never knew how different I was until that moment.

Our meeting ended on a hopeful note. She believed change was coming quickly to business; the accepted definition of leadership was moving from subject matter experts (SMEs) with deep knowledge to leaders like myself who could operate without certainty, as long as we had clarity. What do I mean by clarity without certainty? A good analogy for that is navigating your way north in an unfamiliar environment. Where most people need a compass, a map, GPS, and an arrow pointing them north at all times, I was the type of person who could head north without all that. As long as I knew the general direction I was headed, it was fine. And if plans changed, I could easily adapt.

I may not ever feel like I fit in with the linear thinkers, but I no longer feel like there is something fundamentally dishonest about how I'm presenting myself. And she was right, there has never been a better time than right now for creative thinking and leadership.

We are in an unprecedented time of uncertainty. This is the era of what I like to call the rise of the individual. Martec's Law states that while changes in technology may occur spontaneously and rapidly, organizations change slowly and linearly.

In a white paper on values published by the World Economic Forum in November 2016, this statement stood out: "Given the Fourth Industrial Revolution's extraordinarily fast technological and social change, relying only on government legislation and incentives to ensure the right outcomes is ill-advised. These are likely to be out-of-date or redundant by the time they are implemented."

We see evidence of this everywhere. Technology is moving faster than ever, and yet companies are struggling to get even one pilot program off the ground. Meanwhile, individuals and consumers are driving progress. New generations are reshaping the role of brands in our society, and consumers are demanding brands stand up for what is right. Governments and regulators are being outpaced by a rapidly shifting landscape of cancel culture, whistleblowers, and other spontaneous system disruptions.

In order to transform the businesses that will change the world, we must start with ourselves. We are the individuals who will drive fundamental transformations within our teams and ultimately our organizations. Business leaders at all levels must sift through the overwhelming data, find a path forward, and show others how to take action. To do that, we need to overcome our own imposter syndrome and fears. In short, we need to start trusting ourselves.

To Act or Not to Act

We are taught that, if you don't know something, you're stupid. This couldn't be further from the truth. It means there is a new concept or activity in our lives that we must act on. A frequent statement I hear is, "Don't ask stupid questions," but the *best* question is usually the simplest: why?

We are facing the fastest changing, most complex issues in generations. Whether it is climate action, diversity, equity, or supply chain management, leaders everywhere feel overwhelmed. We are expected to know a broad range of areas, and we aren't capable. I can't tell you how many times I've been in a board or executive meeting and someone has said, "Why would we even do ESG?" as a defense mechanism to avoid learning.

My answer to that is, "Why would you ask that question specifically?"

Once they've told me what their specific issue is, I can answer their question. Asking the simple question "why" allows me to identify the real issue underneath their general questions or declarative dismissive statements. The real issue usually is that they're fearful of coming on too strong or being seen as non-believers when everyone else is nodding their heads in agreement with me.

Back in 2015, I was at a senior leaders meeting. At this time, corporate leaders were focusing on gender equality in leadership. The executive presenter got up and said, "We have 51 percent women in the company, but we know we can do better in senior executive leadership. So, by 2025 we want to have 33 percent women in senior executive leadership."

Everyone clapped.

They had us break out into smaller focus groups and discuss it, but something wasn't sitting right with me. I thought, *why are we celebrating?* Not even 50 percent of our staff would be represented a decade from now. We were still shooting for less than fair.

I was genuinely curious why we were celebrating, so I had to ask the question. And my group agreed with me. After breakouts, we each approached our leadership to address our question. Ultimately, the company decided to target 50 percent instead of 33 percent, and today in 2022 the organization has almost 48.1 percent women in executive leadership. If we had waited there would be leaders today missing out on leadership opportunities because there was no push to have equity.

Another thing to point out is that, in most cases, the moment to directly influence a situation isn't in the heat of that moment. Before we even approached leadership, I actually went up to my boss and then the head of HR and said, "This is our question." I prepared them to answer the question before we even asked it. Granted, it was easier for me to ask that question; I had no direct benefit from it, but that's how important a question can be.

Find time to have those conversations. You don't get to just throw a "question bomb," duck out of the way, and not be part of the solution. I could have stood up after the presenter made their announcement and said, "That's not fair!" It would have been a cheap way of disrupting the conversation, but it most likely wouldn't have gotten the positive outcome I'd wanted if I had proceeded less strategically.

I challenge you as a leader to start thinking of some questions you can start asking, and how to go about that in a way that will open people up to having even more important conversations.

Thanks for the Feedback

Corporations have feedback loops. One of the most influential books for me has been *Thanks for the Feedback* by Douglas Stone and Sheila Heen. We are taught that feedback is something we must adapt to in business, but, in this book, the authors say feedback tells us little about ourselves. We know ourselves: what we're good at, what we're scared of, and what holds us back in our performance. Feedback allows us to see and learn about the people giving it to us—how they see the world and what they value—not us.

After reading this book, I quit reading emails—the area where I had received the most negative feedback during my career.

People who have been working with me a long time know that I never check my email. I text and use social media. If you really need to get ahold of me, call me. This flies in the face of conventional corporate culture where it's pounded into us to be available 24/7 and religiously check all your emails! To this day, some of my colleagues still go through, respond to, and then delete every email they get. For me, this is such a waste of time.

For years, I had the same boss, a very linear thinking and highly introverted manager. My boss was most comfortable communicating through very long, well-thought out emails. This leader would send emails when it was convenient for her and expect that I was always available. You can imagine her feedback to me was consistent: "You don't respond fast enough by email." For more than a decade, I never got the highest performance rating because of this, even though the results of my performance were transformative and industry-leading.

I finally had a conversation with her. I said, "Yes, I know your preference for email, yet it is not the most efficient since we sit next to one another five days a week. There are newer, more efficient ways to communicate, and I'm happy to adapt to some. Can we focus on performance and outcomes?" We talked and negotiated an acceptable communication flow, and as soon as I took back the conversation and set my boundaries, my leadership trajectory took off.

For years I was so worried about my boss thinking I didn't fit into the company's culture. No, I didn't fit into her perception of our team work culture. I was still an innovative leader who could do so much more than answer emails in a timely fashion. The second I started trusting myself and believing in what I was capable of, my fear disappeared. That is when I really started seeing transformation in the business as well as in myself.

I believe we are in the predicament we are in today, struggling to find a way forward, because fears are holding leaders back from action. Not at the team level or system level, we're worried about what others think on a *personal* level. This self-doubt is holding our teams and society back from progressing. We cannot let our worry prevent us from doing the action we were put on the earth to do. In the case of my boss and me, I wasn't thinking of the broader picture; I was holding myself back because I was worried about something as minor as an email and what she would think if I didn't respond to it immediately.

In today's remote work environment, I have seen leaders revert back to a trivial measurement of productivity like email response time or login data. As leaders, we must remain focused on work impact and outcomes, not triviality. If we can truly believe we are capable, care enough about ourselves and others, and take the actions people expect of us, we can take this model and apply it to our team. Shut down the white noise, get clarity, and resolve the biggest issues our people and planet are facing generation after generation.

As leaders, how can we trust ourselves in a way that moves us into action and allows us to practice action? What is it about the world that motivates *you* into action?

ABCs of ESG

Many people like to debate what ESG is and what it isn't—I like action and execution. That means focusing on what it takes to drive change for good, in both impact and permanence. I define sustainability as whatever unleashes people and planet to perform.

However you define it, ESG isn't an emerging framework; it's well established. What is emerging is the complexity of the ESG framework and what it means moving forward. Many are taking ESG as the end-all-be-all, but, in my opinion, it's not. ESG was created to help investors look at a company's operations and performance, not its impact. It's just one framework to enable us to communicate with our stakeholders and eventually consumers.

As leaders, we must transition from the way ESG started—

as a way for investors to ask how a business's operations impact our investment—to the general public's use of ESG today, which is to ask how a business's operations impact society. As empowered individuals, our job is to identify opportunities where ESG can be applied for maximum impact.

The strength of the human brain is its ability to actually collect things and make them relevant for other people.

One time, a direct report and mentor of mine came to me after we'd just gone through a rigorous self and team transformation. She said, "Most people connect dots, Jim. I appreciate you because you collect them and then challenge *us* to connect them." I believe my job is to gather various dots so leaders can see why they need to act right now. Since then, I've taken the moniker on: I'm a collector of dots!

As leaders, it's our job to go out into the system where the white noise can be overwhelming and pull out specific dots so that we can start to galvanize ourselves and our teams to take action and affect change. We set the stage for the urgency to act right now. I believe it's important that we bring the various dots together so all stakeholders—customers, employees, suppliers, and investors—can see why ESG is important.

It's true that investors are a bit more savvy nowadays. At the same time, when we see old frameworks that aren't relevant, it is our job to speak up. For instance, take the healthcare sector. One of the leading ESG standards does not include DEI as a relevant topic for healthcare companies. Their reasoning is that diversity, equity, and inclusion aren't relevant to healthcare because healthcare companies need to focus on health. The fact is, the standard doesn't take into consideration the long-standing racial inequalities in healthcare. It was COVID-19 that reinforced why DEI is a critical factor in healthcare, which became a key topic during the pandemic.

We've put systems in place to provide a false sense of security that all is working well. Those are precisely the things we have to start changing. The traditional ESG framework says that DEI doesn't matter in the healthcare industry, but society is telling us, *oh no, it matters*. That is where we have to step in and both collect and connect the dots for our stakeholders.

As leaders, we have to balance multiple stakeholders and ultimately remember why we are here—we want to radically change our industries for all. If we don't have DEI baked into our operations, we won't fulfill this goal.

Now, I was in healthcare for 25 years, but, regardless of industry, if a framework says a particular ESG topic doesn't matter, you as a leader still need to assess how it applies in the current context. For example, if you're in education, access to education is important. There may be historically excluded communities for whom you need to consider how these communities are impacted and what needs to change to ensure equal opportunity and access. Or you may be on a college or corporate campus evaluating greenhouse gas emissions. Just because someone tells you not to worry about something, you still need to assess the situation for the way things should be done today, not how they've traditionally been done. Trust yourself, and trust your gut.

If you are only interested in protecting the status quo and preserving frameworks that have been proven ineffective, this book isn't for you. If you are looking to unleash people and the planet to perform, then read on.

2

In Business We Trust

There was a time in my career when I was asked to take on DEI as a leader, and I didn't know what the acronym meant. Not only that, but I was struggling with the concept of my role, especially when it related to privilege. I didn't feel like I was raised with privilege or like I had an easy road in life—until someone cared enough to educate me. I learned there are many power systems in the world, and I directly benefited from being born into some of the most dominant. I became a global thought leader in this space because I cared enough to learn and I'm able to walk my talk. Though I have come a long way, I'm not perfect.

The other night, we were with our son at the home of dear

family friends and their three boys. Their oldest boy was talking about how he didn't like the work he was doing at his first job. Without a second thought, I turned to his father and asked, "Do you like your job?" He responded no. We talked about this for a bit, and then the mom, standing next to me, said quietly, "I don't always like my work."

Later, when I was in the car, I realized that I had made a grave mistake: I instinctively left the mom out of the conversation because the "men folk" were talking about work. Here was my friend, an educator, and I had minimized her as a professional—in front of four young men no less. I immediately texted her, "I'm sorry for being a misogynistic ass." I was so embarrassed, I even offered to speak to her sons about what had happened. She quickly returned my text with a call. We talked and were both shocked at how frequently this happens. She was extremely touched and appreciative.

I have literally been up on a global stage at SXSW presenting as a thought leader on DEI and the role of male advocates. I was not walking my talk when I excluded my friend from the work conversation over dinner. It's hard to earn trust. But owning up to it when you fail is an important part of keeping your word with others. The point is, companies are going to break trust and fail because people fail. But the great thing about trust is that you can always build it back up again by taking responsibility for your words and actions.

One example of this that comes to mind is "Dieselgate," the Volkswagen emissions scandal. In 2015, the US EPA issued a notice of violation to Volkswagen; the company had intentionally programmed their vehicles to misrepresent their emissions.

Volkswagen's initial response was to immediately do a recall. They suspended the head of brand development and all the employees directly responsible for the mistake, paid one of the largest fines in history, and settled the case. Volkswagen then made a commitment to go fully electric in Europe by 2033. The point I'm trying to make is that companies break and rebuild trust all the time.

When the UN laid out its Sustainable Development Goals (the SDGs) in 2015, they were designed for the country level; the SDGs were meant for countries to establish best practices and deliver impact. What we have seen instead are global powers turning inward due to populist and nationalist movements like "Brexit" in the United Kingdom and "Make America Great Again" in the United States.

As the world faces significant change, we have seen nations focus on securing their own interests through protectionism. World powers have stopped helping developing countries, jeopardizing the promise and progress of the SDGs. In this environment, stakeholders have turned to business as the only arena with money and influence willing to operate across borders to address some of the biggest challenges we face today.

This gap of cross-border leadership has society looking for who will lead the charge to fix the problems. Because corporations have financial interest in finding expanded markets and influencing policy, stakeholders are asking business leaders to take a stand on social issues like MeToo, BLM, Net Zero Pledges, and climate action. Now that we're living with this concept of "in business we trust," the question is can we trust businesses to do what they say they will? Are companies turning aspirations into operations? Or are businesses making ESG commitments and then lobbying for different interests?

For instance, you may have seen "Big Pharma" CEOs in the news lately saying they want responsible pricing and equal access to healthcare around the world. That is great. But simultaneously, the industry lobbying association does not support the ability of the U.S. Medicare program to negotiate drug pricing because it will "stifle innovation." Yet, the United States is the only developed country that does not have the federal government negotiate its prescription drug prices. Obviously, if pharma CEOs *say* they want responsible pricing, non-negotiation with the U.S. government is not the way.

The truth is, the industry does not want strong price controls in its largest and most profitable market. If "Big Pharma" wants to earn our trust, the solution to equitable healthcare is not uncontrolled drug pricing in the U.S. I'm not saying this is the end-all-be-all solution to the healthcare crisis in the U.S. Fast, simple solutions to complex problems are often proven wrong. As it relates to U.S. healthcare, we have issues on multiple levels with insurance companies, pharmacies, PBMs, and large provider networks. It's a whole host of things. But when the industry's CEOs tout access to healthcare and affordable pricing while their Government Affairs teams are lobbying against negotiating with Medicare, that's a prime example of aspirations and operations not matching.

Another example is the beverage industry and plastic bottles. Major soft drink companies boast of recyclable containers and bottles, yet, while 90 percent of all aluminum is getting recycled, it's the exact opposite for plastic. Humans use about 1.2 million plastic bottles per minute, and 91 percent of them aren't recycled. In 2020, the Senior Vice President and Communications and Sustainability Officer at Coca-Cola was quoted at WEF as saying, "Our customers want single-use plastic bottles." She also stated that Coca-Cola would continue to use plastic so as not to alienate consumers and hurt sales. The company has committed to switch to 50 percent recycled materials by 2030.

In response to this position, Piplsy, a consumer insights expert, did a quick survey on Coca-Cola's plastic dilemma. Of the more than 32,000 Americans surveyed, 51 percent said they would still buy Coke in a heavier, non-resealable container and 42 percent of respondents said they think Coca-Cola should use eco-friendly packaging, like aluminum or glass.

Companies like Coca-Cola have a strategy to be within arm's reach of everyone on the planet. My expectation of a company with that strategy is, if you're within arm's reach of getting your product into their hands, how are you doing that ethically by collecting that container back? The point is, plastic is harming us, and just because Coca-Cola's research suggests consumers like it doesn't mean that a responsible shift would hurt their sales. There's enough science to reasonably conclude that those of us who use plastic have to rethink our business operations, including packaging, so that they match our aspirations.

In 2019, Edelman published its Trust Barometer Global Report which found that the current U.S. consumer trust in brands is at 54 percent. Yet, 76 percent of people also say that CEOs should take the lead on change rather than waiting for government to impose it. People expect businesses to step up, and most of us would agree trust is the new social contract.

Some companies are very good at fostering trust; companies like Domino's and Southwest Airlines are scoring higher with consumers because of their willingness to build a relationship of trust with their audience. (Southwest Airlines is always consistent with its culture and even when serious disruption happens like in 2022, the company relies on that culture to get through. Even as a non-loyal customer, I love that I know what the Southwest Airlines brand is about and that is why it has a radically loyal following.) While other companies, like the aforementioned examples in "Big Pharma" and the beverage industry, are still lagging behind in their efforts to earn trust.

Even Edelman, the creator of the Trust Barometer, has struggled with trust. They had a hand in the misinformation campaigns of oil and gas companies, working with ExxonMobil and Shell while simultaneously making public statements in favor of sustainability. In 2021, they had to issue a mea culpa and reevaluate their efforts. This isn't to say that Edelman is a horrible organization. They have 6,000 employees worldwide; that's a small city. There's always going to be crime in a small town. Any big company is going to have circumstances like this. The reality is, trust is going to be broken, and that is precisely why it is important for businesses to follow a simple trust model that they can quickly come back to and use to reorient and to prove that they are doing what they say they will.

Walk Your Talk

Once, I was presenting to an executive team to get their buy-in on electric vehicles. When they asked me what I drove, I responded, "Electric," and that changed the conversation. It's important to note that I also knew they wouldn't ask me for how long (I had only been driving my electric vehicle for about four weeks). But it was enough to minimize any objection they were going to raise based on my own behavior. It's about walking your talk. I wasn't asking these executives to do something that I hadn't done before. As a business executive you must prove you're doing what you said you would do.

As businesses start the transition into the decade of our lives—the 2020s—trust is the most critical factor. And yet, overcoming shareholder skepticism and gaining consensus on vital topics has been almost impossible to achieve. There's a reason for this.

The largest issues we as business leaders are trying to address quite literally are polarizing—climate change, DEI, equal pay for women—because the basic concepts that most people agree on have been politicized. Looking at the headlines today as we gear up for the 2022 midterm elections, ESG itself is at the forefront of controversy. Trust isn't partisan; trust transcends the polarization we face in our communities and around the world. That makes earning trust foundational to how we move forward to save the planet and ourselves.

With trust in media and government at an all-time low and the evolution of fake news statements and alternate truths, people are looking for direction and support. Companies must work to drive change and be willing to lead instead of waiting for policy. If we, as leaders, can steer the conversation from talking about Critical Race Theory and climate change to talking about trust, even the most polarized people will understand and champion trust.

In my opinion, the biggest shift we need to make is getting away from all these hot button topics and getting back to answering one simple question: do our stakeholders trust us or not?

Companies are writing a new social contract that stipulates what they care about as a company and why. This is about business walking the talk, and the more trust we have, the better business functions and the less polarized we will be.

Warren Buffett said it can take 20 years to build trust—you can lose it in five minutes today.

In short, do what you say you will.

Right from the Start

When I say "right from the start," what I mean is that companies today don't get to start out badly.

A new business today should not need pay and equity initiatives. They should be starting off with fair and equitable pay, not starting out with unfair pay and then expecting kudos for closing the pay gap. The whole concept of taking time to fix ESG issues isn't acceptable anymore. The starting line has moved—and it's behind us.

Business is the most trusted entity in the world, ahead of governmental, religious, and educational systems. If we want more trust, we must be more transparent. Seeing is believing.

This includes good reporting practices and accessible data for all stakeholders. It can also involve leveraging social media and the corporate website to share information about the status of various topics of importance. Companies must disclose targets, timelines, and progress on vital issues. As leaders, we should explore what trust means to businesses and why. Do our aspirations match the operations? And, more importantly, if business is the most trusted entity, what do people trust your business to do?

Because we must master multiple topics depending on the needs of the business and the stakeholders that are depending on us, it can be overwhelming and difficult to know where to start. Let's start with the basics of trust. How can you be inspired to step into the trust model of can-care-do?

3

Can, Care, Do

I keep coming back to the example of "Big Pharma," and there are two reasons why. The obvious one is this is where I have spent most of my career. Second, I'm a practitioner. I spend my days on the front lines of business. I am not a member of academia or a consultancy firm sitting around dreaming up models; I spend my days proving action beats inaction every time. This is what I saw at AstraZeneca: both leaders and the industry stepped up when the world stopped. This multinational pharmaceutical company trusted its knowledge of human health and took action during an unprecedented time, the COVID-19 global pandemic.

Behind the backdrop of a warming planet and a global

COVID crisis, AstraZeneca did what it does best: address the health of the people and the planet. It delivered the most widely used vaccine on the market during the pandemic. The company also stuck to its principles and made sure its vaccine was designed not just to help wealthy developed countries, but low to middle income countries and the entire world. Through maintaining strong aspirations, this company demonstrated that it cares because it understands that a healthier planet equals healthier people. AstraZeneca has proven it will do what it says it will.

As a leader who has been in the thick of chaos, I've been striving to deliver a simplified model of trust to other corporate leaders that has demonstrated results. What it boils down to is my model of *can, care, do*. I know this model works because I've seen it work not just for me but for everyone. When the pandemic took off, our Chief Medical Officer and I were tasked with maintaining operations both while we continued to supply our current products to patients in need and while the company simultaneously began developing one of the first global COVID vaccines.

"Big Pharma" gets a bad rap for drug pricing, yet the industry is pivotal to addressing human health. This was never more evident than during COVID. Businesses led the way out of the pandemic, and COVID, with all its tragedy, showed the quality of mankind and what we are truly capable of. This is why I am so active in getting leaders to act right now. I have seen firsthand that, if we trust ourselves, we can influence our families, our friends, and our teams to transform ourselves and to change the world. We can't always fix the system at a system level. If

COVID highlighted anything, it was that real change is possible when we do our part to address the overall problem as individuals first.

This is why people trust business. Because when businesses take bold action, they can change, or even save, the world.

It is important to emphasize that I'm not a scientist—I wasn't developing vaccines. AstraZeneca wasn't developing vaccines *either*, prior to the pandemic. But because it is a science led company that centers around health, I saw colleagues taking on tasks they'd never taken on before, transforming their teams to solve a global problem. I saw leaders raising their hands saying, "I haven't done that before, but I will try." And ultimately, they proved that they were capable of rising to the occasion. They innovated, studied, and produced a product that was needed right now. That's the can, care, do model in action.

No matter what the circumstances, it all comes down to one thing—can we achieve this? There are so many topics that businesses can worry about, but we have to distill them down and focus on what a company should be working on—where a company can make its biggest impact when the time comes.

Leaders often ask me, "Where do I start?"

My answer is to start with what you know, what you're capable of, and do it.

Weight No More

In 2015, I was asked to become the head of the Environmental, Health and Safety team at my company. I knew I had the chops and the technical skills, and the knowledge I could learn, but I had some serious doubts around walking the talk—because I was obese! Of course, I said yes, I'll take it on. But my personal challenge was my weight.

At 6'4", I've always been a big guy. Men get away with carrying a few extra pounds. But if I was genuinely going to lead the health function of a company, I knew I had to get my health under control. It was the only way to prove that I was capable and that I cared about others enough to want to motivate them to start on their own health journey. So, I started working with a dietician. I shed 90 pounds over a year and a half. That's the weight of my youngest child. I literally lost the equivalent of a small person—talk about losing baby weight!

To inspire my team and a company focused on human health, I had to focus on myself.

Once you learn the can, care, do model, it's very easy to adopt. Take my case, for instance. I knew I had the skills, knowledge, and willingness to lose the weight—that's "can." "Care" meant I was focused on the outcome—I wanted to inspire a team inside a company to drive health—and I even had to prove that I cared enough about *myself* to do this. Finally, the "do" was the action I chose to take, hand to mouth, changing the way I was eating. This is when I reinforced for myself that the model of can, care, do actually works. Not only that, I truly saw the three levels of trust in action, and the interplay between self, team, and system.

In this case, the aspiration was there, and that aspiration was rooted in the employees' health. I had a small team: about 17 direct reports and five or six team members focused on the health part of our team's remit. We were dedicated to taking on 70,000 employees and helping them address human determinants of health, like smoking cessation, responsible alcohol consumption, exercise, and diet. We started to work with local sites to subsidize the cost of healthier food so that it was just as attractive to get a salad as it was to get a bag of chips. We were demonstrating to the employees what healthy food options looked like. We also made sure the employees had access to water more readily, not just vending machines with sugary drinks. Next, we took on movement, one of the key aspects of health. We utilized Virgin Pulse, one of the largest corporate health initiatives, and became one of the biggest users driving movement within the company. This initiative, coupled with our innovative introduction of walking meetings, ensured that our colleagues were getting their steps in.

For me to lead a global health division for a global health company, I knew I had to prove that I could do the job, that I cared, and that I would live up to my word. Since then, I've gone up and down 10-15 pounds at any given time, but I'm always focused on health. When I start over carrying weight, I know I need to balance that out and take care of myself.

Missing is Action

I always try to figure out what's missing. And what's missing most of the time in developing trust is action—missing is action (ironically MIA).

When I'm assessing a situation where a leader says they can't act, it's one of three reasons: either they don't believe they can do it, they don't have others' interests at heart, or there are barriers that are preventing that action from taking place.

For instance, when I say I'm going to treat everyone equally, people trust that I will. But the systems we find ourselves in are operating the way they were intended, and, whether we like it or not, they are keeping people marginalized. As of 2022, only 8.8 percent of the fortune 500 companies have female CEOs, and we aren't changing the way we recruit. Savoy recently released their 2022 Most Influential Black Executives list with a record number of fortune 500 CEOs, yet it is only a measly six leaders. That's 1 percent of the industry. Part of your purpose as a leader is and should be driving equity. You will not be able to navigate teams or systems when there are clear barriers to everyone having equal opportunity to lead.

In 2020, the CEO of Wells Fargo Charles Scharf infamously blamed not meeting their diversity goals on the "very limited pool of black talent to recruit from." It's important to note he also said this during one of the most important civil rights protests that has happened in our country to date. The irony of this forced me to start thinking about what I could do as an individual to bring more equity into my own banking experience. So, I set out on a mission to find the more than qualified people out there who weren't being represented.

I began by calling financial institutions and telling them that I was looking for a financial planner who was non-white or female, and ideally both. I can't tell you how many times I was told, "We're working on it," and I simply said, "Call me when you have it," knowing they would never get back to me. Or I heard, "We don't discriminate against our advisors." The irony is that they *do* discriminate, but they're only willing to do it when it suits their needs, not the needs of the customers who are supplying the money. I realized that until customers started asking for equity, the same executives would have the same excuses and companies would continue to operate as they always had.

Finally, Fidelity matched me up with an advisor in a virtual meeting who met my requested requirements. To my surprise, when I joined the call, a man's voice was on the line! I immediately said, "Before we continue, I need to know if you're a white man? If you are, I'm going to end the call."

The man chuckled, "No, no, I've been warned. She wasn't able to make it. I'm of Hispanic descent."

I said, "Thank you, let's keep talking."

Within four minutes of talking, he asked me where I went to school, and I told him Missouri. He said his wife studied business there and, not only that, she graduated the same year as I did. Then he mentioned the name of her high school. I started to have a sneaking suspicion, so I asked, "Are you married to . . . ?"

I heard, "Hey, come here!" He called for his wife, who was a dear friend of mine from college, to join the call. He admitted that, before the call, he had told his wife that it would be an interesting discussion since it was a white man making these demands. We all had a good laugh.

Not only did I get someone more qualified, but I got to reconnect with a dear friend. The moral of the story is that the system can work when we ask for what we want and if those of us in power positions leverage our power for good.

You are not helpless; you have more control than you realize.

When something is "missing in action" and you don't know why, always come back to self. Define what self and team can look like for you, even if your team is a family. Make sure you understand the topic, that you care about others enough, and that you're walking the talk. Transformation doesn't happen from the outside in; it starts in small pockets with a grassroots approach. At the center of my model, self will always be there; if I can transform myself, I can inspire my team, and we can transform the world.

Model of Trust

It is one thing to understand and define trust. It is something else entirely to make trust a verb and put trust in action at one of three levels: self, team, and system.

The three levels can scale up and down. For example, the model might represent an individual (self) as part of a business unit (team) within a company (system). The interplay could also be a business (self) operating within an industry (team) as part of the economy (system). Regardless of the scope, each level is dependent on relationships. If trust doesn't exist, the relationship will break down.

Another important factor is the flow of trust: from self to team to system and back. Our built systems are created to help individuals find where they belong and the role they play. Often, the role is based on how the system was designed. A significant push for me to bring the can, care, do model to life is to help challenge this position. Just as I had an awakening over how my non-linear thinking is an asset in a swiftly changing world, my goal is to inspire you, the reader, to trust yourself and to take action.

Trust: Creating the building blocks of action

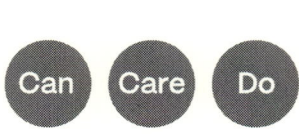

When **Can, Care,** and **Do** come together, something interesting happens. Trust is formed. Trust is the connective tissue that makes positive action possible. It creates the building blocks for a successful self, team, and system.

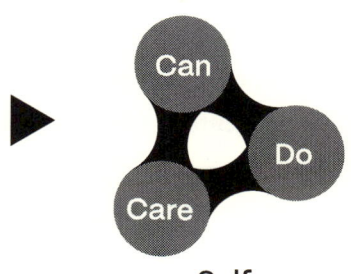
Self

Team

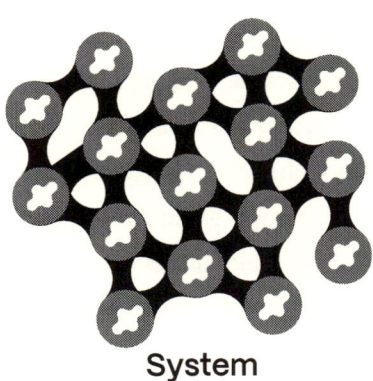
System

Satisfied that my "can" was covered, I turned my attention to "care" and "do". I realized that by simply changing four letters from reduce to *remove*, it would show why it mattered. Instead of mitigating the amount of greenhouse gasses, we would now be completely eliminating greenhouse gas from our operations.

They'd come so far, and now I was asking them to push a little further and to drive stronger action that was more aligned with the team's real aspirations to save our planet. Changing four letters sounds easy, but it was challenging to convince them. The team had already done significant work to get to the STBI target. The last thing any team wants is for the target to be moved. But it was my job to show them how we could do both; we not only could, but must do more to a further degree, or 1.5 degrees to be exact. By doing this, we would be forming the trust needed to transform ourselves and the planet. As it turned out, that minor tweak is what got AstraZeneca to shift its focus to the first net zero program, which we launched at DAVOS that same spring when COVID had shut the world down.

I'm happy to say that by 2019, AstraZeneca was one of the first companies in the world to launch a net zero approved target, endorsed by SBTI in Q1 2021, and Bloomberg recognized the company for having the most comprehensive and progressive environmental plan of a publicly traded company.

My lesson is simple—trust begins at any phase of the can, care, do model. Pick one and go.

PART 1
CAN

4

Why Do You Exist?

Milton Friedman once famously quipped, "The business of business is business."

With today's limited resources, you aren't just in business to create wealth anymore; you have to have a social purpose beyond profits. In 2020, the National Association of Corporate Directors (NACD) released its annual Governance Challenge research with a focus on the board's role in drafting company strategy. The most staggering result from the survey was that 86 percent of sitting directors indicated that, over the next five years, their companies' existing strategies will become completely irrelevant.

This reinforces a key finding from the research that one of

the biggest challenges businesses face is, "how to keep the strategy and mission resilient in the face of threats that have the potential to make existing business models obsolete [. . .]," a fact which places trust and the dimension of "can" front and center for businesses. For existing organizations, this means you must re-examine every aspect of your operations, including your right to exist.

For startups, the next 1,000 unicorns will be companies that understand from the beginning that they have *social* value. They are here to add value to society beyond quarterly earnings, they recognize the importance of the empowered individual, and they treat the planet and people as a stakeholder.

The challenge sits with existing companies. Big, multinational organizations and the complexity of changing business models need to be aligned with making and sustaining social impact. As daunting as it sounds, the groundwork is being laid by innovators today. The reality is that adoption must be faster for more of us if we want to save our planet.

As of 2021, IKEA launched its Green Friday Buy Back & Resell program in 33 stores across the U.S. as well as a new 'Sustainable Living Shop' with discounts and offers on sustainable products during November, its busiest shopping season. The company has also proposed making a commitment to not produce anymore new furniture. The idea is to use the buyback program exclusively and reuse the pieces that are already made. Similarly, H&M launched a recycled clothing program that collected 18,800 tons of unwanted clothes and textiles in 2020—the equivalent of 94 million T-shirts—but they haven't stopped generating T-shirts under $10. They need to fix that.

I applaud the effort of a company directly addressing the social burden of its products. But why stop there? More than a decade ago, a leading tobacco company made a commitment to create less harmful alternatives to cigarettes. In March 2021, during its virtual investor day, the company announced it would become a majority smoke-free company by 2025 and acknowledged the smoke-free future they are driving is less harmful. The stark reality is that the company should not applaud itself for doing less bad. The real question I offer the company and its industry is *why do we even have a tobacco industry*? Tobacco doesn't serve a positive social purpose and the industry's socio-economic harm significantly outweighs any benefits. As an agricultural-based industry, tobacco companies could pivot operations to address one of society's biggest threats, food insecurity, and still have economic benefits through reclaiming soil and producing food instead of harmful tobacco.

Make no mistake, I don't believe companies should exist if they can't demonstrate that they are capable of stepping up. If IKEA can get to the point where they can say let's recycle what we already have instead of producing new furniture, H&M can stop clogging up landfills with fast fashion, and a tobacco company can move from less harm to potentially doing good by converting tobacco fields into sustainable farms, we can get most brands to do the same.

Part of the reason for writing this book was that I believe we are going to start having these difficult conversations among various stakeholders, including the consumer and investor communities. In light of the fact that we are moving into this critical period, if the reason your company exists isn't aligned with one of the 169 targets of the SDG's, you are only driving consumption and using limited global resources. Companies that don't adapt are going to start being confronted with questions of their right to existence.

In short, does your company have a social purpose? And once you've identified that purpose, are you capable of proving to your stakeholders that you can fulfill this purpose? Will you be part of those who contribute to the solution, even ahead of higher profits, or continue to ignore the problems?

No Representation Without Taxation

We've already established that ESG goes beyond how a company's operations impact money. But it can also affect supply chains, infrastructure, and the global communities we live in and share.

Since its peak in the late 1960s, the U.S. federal corporate tax rate has continued to decline. In 2021, nearly one in five fortune 100 companies paid nothing or next to nothing in federal taxes. Legally, companies can follow the current tax code and minimize or avoid paying taxes. Yet, those same companies have ESG goals and commitments, making tax avoidance difficult to reconcile with the idea of being a good corporate citizen. If a company does not pay its fair share of taxes, is it truly good? How do these companies help support our society in the post-Friedman world? Are they providing better infrastructure like a resilient green power grid or maintained rails, roads, and bridges for product distribution?

This very topic of corporate tax[1] and the need to invest in our infrastructure made headlines in February 2022. On February 4, Jeff Bezos, the world's second wealthiest person and founder/CEO of Amazon, offered to cover the cost to dismantle Netherland's iconic and historic Koningshaven Bridge so his gigayacht could leave the manufacturers port. Just three days later on February 7, as President Biden was scheduled to head to Pittsburgh to discuss the importance of securing our national infrastructure, a bridge collapsed in Pittsburgh, PA. The same day, the Institute on Taxation and Economic Policy issued a press release stating that Amazon had record breaking profits in 2021 and avoided paying more than $5B in federal taxes that same year. Though these stories are not directly linked, the backlash Bezos and Amazon faced was very real. If Bezos was willing to fork over millions to dismantle a bridge for his own benefit, imagine what $5B could do to help strengthen the US infrastructure, including in Pittsburgh, PA where more than one thousand of his employees live and work.

It used to be the case that companies could destroy a supply chain at will; the attitude was if it's not working, it's gone. Today, with globalization, you often have a single source for the origination of your product; you can't just cut it out of your business model or fire it. Corporations must partner with their supply chains and bring them up to speed on how they need to operate. For instance, Unilever has committed to paying a fair and livable wage to its workforce, including to employees throughout

---

1 https://www.forbes.com/sites/noahkirsch/2017/11/09/the-3-richest-americans-hold-more-wealth-than-bottom-50-of-country-study-finds/?sh=267b3d273cf8

the supply chain, and, in turn, they had to increase the amount they were paying their suppliers in order to meet that criteria. In 2021, the company was awarded its first global independent accreditation as a living wage employer. That's how aspirations turn into operations.

For so long, businesses only cared about investors and shareholder value. This is shareholder primacy. Today, companies must prove they care about more than just investors. We can no longer afford to neglect our employees and partners, our cities, or our communities, or just generally not care.

Born to Build

Referring back to my life's work, which I talked about in Chapter One, I had to evolve my purpose and answer the question: why do I exist?

In graduate school, we developed purpose statements. Mine was "to create a barrier-free environment so those who are willing can be who they need to be in the world." Sounds great, right? That purpose served me for many, many years, until the day when someone said, "Boy, I wish I were a white guy who could always remove barriers for others and never saw one myself."

By stating this purpose, I was unknowingly alienating those around me who saw nothing but barriers throughout their day. What I actually wanted was for everyone to have what I had, so I had to flip my priorities. This forced me to dig deeper and create a new purpose which was that I was born to "build our better." Because of the positions of power which I was born into, I got to change the system from within. It has nothing to do with individuals who are willing; we all have the right to a barrier-free environment. In order to benefit more people quickly, I had to adapt. Now, I proudly say that I was born to build our better.

When I'm sitting in a meeting and I hear people saying things that aren't congruent with my purpose—building our better—I speak up. Because not everyone is afforded this luxury, it's my job to speak up as an advocate and not wait for those hurt by the barrier to approach me and ask for my support. By that point, it is too late.

When I say it can be done, I'm speaking from experience. Just as I had to dig deeper to find my true purpose, companies *can* do better.

For instance, ORSTED is ranked one of the most sustainable energy companies in the world, and they stay at the top because they demonstrate that they *can*.

ORSTED used to be one of Europe's largest oil, gas, and coal extractors, with 85 percent of its power coming from fossil fuels; it was a true power conglomerate. It made a commitment to 85 percent power from renewable sources by 2040, and, not only that, it hit its target 20 years ahead of schedule. Today, they have committed to net zero emissions by 2040.

In this case, the CEO was the individual inside catalyzing change. What is ORSTED's benefit to society? Power. But its employees knew they couldn't keep doing it the old way, so they moved to clean energy like solar, hydro, and wind. Today, they are the first energy company in the world with a science-based net zero target, competing against companies like Chevron,

Shell Oil, and gas companies who haven't converted to clean energy—and this company has already flipped. Now, they still provide energy but in an ethical and sustainable way.

Understanding why you exist and taking care of that purpose responsibly is the essence of the "can" part of the can, care, do model.

"It can't be done" is something that companies say when they are focused on the wrong things.

Many companies will say things like, "We follow these multiple SDG's. We're focused on inequalities. We're focused on eliminating homelessness and hunger." But when you look closer, none of these issues are directly tied to their core business. In my work, I find broad approaches often show an immaturity in the company's sustainability program and commitment to making the most meaningful impact. In the end, a company is ignoring the fact that it is not actually addressing the existential problem the business is contributing to most.

Companies are trying to be all things to everyone when they should really figure out why they exist first. Once they've demonstrated that they're capable, then they can find their purpose and values through that lens.

If companies like ORSTED can handle the renewable energy problem, it inspires other sectors to focus on matters where they can drive the most impact instead of everyone trying to address something outside of our expertise. Healthcare companies can focus on health and wellbeing while food companies can focus on ending hunger. Oil and gas companies can talk about how good they are in their daily operations, but, let's be honest, at the end of the day fossil fuels are the dominant cause of global heating and the lack of transition to renewable energy is killing the planet.

I appreciate the brands that are trying, but I want to know—why do you exist? What social good do you provide the world? Business must have a social purpose and contribute a benefit other than consumption. At our current rate of consumption, we will need 1.7 planets to sustain that consumption, and we only have one. So, unless you have a backup planet in mind, it's time for us to start having these conversations.

What the World Needs Now

Once a company or individual understands why they matter, the next challenge is figuring out what you are trying to do. What is the goal? More critically, what is the desired impact?

First, clarify the purpose. Sit down and define your purpose in as much detail as possible, identifying what differentiates your purpose and what makes your contribution to that purpose unique. Why would consumers, employees, and investors be interested in you?

Next, articulate this purpose. Write down your intentions and revisit the document regularly to keep it fresh in your mind. Companies should communicate this purpose broadly and regularly—reminding their employees, stakeholders, and customers why the organization exists and what they seek to accomplish. This will help workers have a line of sight from their work to the importance of the company's purpose overall. Companies can leverage this purpose statement to unify the workforce and energize stakeholders around a common cause.

Companies wondering how to deliver on the long-term stakeholder goals should start by asking the questions, "We know why we exist, but where can we make our greatest impact? What would the world lose if our company disappeared?"

Whether you're a business leader or a consumer or a CEO, figure out what is the differentiating benefit you bring and where can you make the greatest impact. This idea shapes your strategy, inspires your people, and steers teams and the company at critical moments. In this decade, companies must move from aspirations to operations. Act and deliver. In short, if your business is not helping address the biggest challenges we face, you will find yourself answering the questions of why and if your organization needs to exist.

5

The Purpose *of* Purpose

It seems like the word "purpose" is in business headlines everywhere. While writing this chapter, I decided to look up my chapter title to make sure that the title did not mean something else in slang or cultural context. I was fascinated by what I found, like this *Harvard Business Review* article entitled *What is the Purpose of Your Purpose?*[2]

In the article, the authors urge executives to "articulate a role for their companies beyond profit making," and lay out three areas where a company can define its purpose: competence, culture, and cause. What shocked me about this article was that it

---

2 https://hbr.org/2022/03/what-is-the-purpose-of-your-purpose

was written in April of 2022. I would have loved to have seen something like this come out in the late 70s, 80s, or even the 90s when we had time to focus on culture and competence.

Today, there is only one area of business that can actually make a difference and that's cause. Competence and culture are intrinsic. It's just how you operate a business. But the question remains—why do you exist? And it isn't because you have a "cool" company culture or a product that makes people feel good. You exist because of the benefit you bring to the world at large.

Everyone goes to *HBR* for business, but even in 2022, the authors are still looking at the role of purpose in business, instead of looking at the role of business in society. In my opinion, this view is outdated. Looking inward at how you operate is no longer acceptable. We have to work within the context of the system because that's the state of play that we're in. Businesses are part of the built environment where humans interact with nature, society, and the planet. By not connecting the context to our cause, we are pretending these things can still exist separately, and they simply can't.

For so long, culture has been at the forefront of industry thought leadership, especially in tech. It was a "bro culture" that only furthered the systems to work the way they were designed. What happens when a company is acquired? We suddenly have private equity investors coming in and stripping down its culture to make a company profitable. Culture gets sacrificed quickly. That's why we want things rooted in cause, because when it's rooted there, your culture must serve the cause.

If your startup is in the unicorn phase and you think your company culture is unique enough to allow you to exist—you're a social club, not a company. We need companies to be creating products and cultures that serve a purpose.

What motivates me, and the reason why I wrote this book, is trying to help others understand that we cannot afford not to be singularly focused on social impact. Because that is the only sphere that matters. The benefit of having a cause-based purpose is that it will drive responsible products and an inclusive culture. It works because you're putting why you care about others front and center. If you only focus on competence or culture, you will never get to the existential purpose of existing, which takes us right back to 'why do you exist?'

Creating a product people want to buy without thinking of the impact of that product on the planet is how you end up with "Oil and Gas" fighting for their industry's survival instead of our planet's survival. It's how you end up with the next single use product. Just because it's making a profit doesn't make it right. Being rooted in cause will drive both your culture and product development.

Every Vote Counts

Throughout our careers, we're conditioned not to focus on ourselves. When we accomplish something in business, we're told to speak about it in terms of "we did this." And yet, the 'I' matters. Trust in action only happens when we find the I—when we discover *ourselves* in self, team, and system.

My whole life, I knew I wanted to be a politician; it's how I was raised. My grandpa was involved in local politics and served as the senior member of his party for many years. I have fond memories of my grandpa and me helping out congressmen, campaigning, or handing out buttons at parades. Thanks to the influence of my grandpa, I did everything to put myself on the right path for a career in state politics.

In high school, I was class president. When it came time to choose a college, I chose the University of Missouri because that was our state's flagship campus—and what better way to represent my state! Later, I ran for student senate at-large and had to convince the current members of the Missouri Students Association to vote for me. I distinctly remember at the end of the race finding out I had the highest number of votes—but I also noticed one person didn't vote for me. (It forever bugged me because I had no idea who that person was or why I couldn't get that vote.)

From the student senate, I began to leverage my network and made the right connections. One summer, I found myself volunteering in Presidential Personnel at the White House. All my hard work, planning, and networking launched me into the center of U.S. politics, right where I thought I wanted to be. Finding myself in the midst of the White House entourage, I realized it wasn't what I wanted. Politics wasn't for me. Ironically, 1600 Pennsylvania Avenue was where my path to politics sadly ended. I had to go back to Missouri with a degree and no job.

Luckily, I trusted the system and the system helped me find a new career path.

I met with the Dean of the Business School and mentioned I wasn't doing politics. He said, "Great, I have a recruiter for you to meet." A month later, I had a job at a pharmaceutical company doing sales. I had no idea a pharmaceutical industry existed, let alone a job doing sales. It was a world I knew nothing about.

The reason I wanted to get into politics was because I thought the best way to positively influence human behavior was through policy. Today, I spend much of my time on policy, but the emphasis is on grassroots action. The desire to shape behavior in a positive way still drives me, but the expression of that drive is very different. Luckily, the system guided me to a position where I can actually have a greater impact than if I were in politics. Martec's Law defines a conundrum for leaders in the 21st century. We know that policy is lagging and that grass roots is actually where it's at. Focusing on individual action has helped me drive change quickly within organizations by simply getting employees engaged.

In my early twenties, I was lucky I accepted that I didn't know it all. Looking back, I'm so glad I trusted the system to help me find my path. It's these reflections that helped me build the foundations for *Trust in Action* and understand the role I played in teams, in the system, and in trust. This thinking is why I focus on breaking convention and finding the 'I' in team. Trust starts with each of us and our own ability to confidently believe I can, I care, I do.

Twenty years later, I finally solved the mystery of who didn't vote for me. I was at a cocktail reunion party with college friends, and sitting across the table from me was a lifelong friend. I casually mentioned my run for student senate and how I never figured out who it was who didn't vote for me. "It still gets me," I said.

My friend's eyes immediately darted over to my wife sitting next to me, and my friend said, "You never told him??"

I turned and looked at my wife Emily and said, "You never told me *what?*"

Turns out, my wife didn't vote for me because she didn't think that I cared. We weren't dating yet, and I made a classic blunder. On the eve of the election, I greeted her and said, "Nice to meet you," but I had already met her the weekend before. In the rush of the campaign, I had forgotten. She knew I was capable, but the foundations of trust hadn't been established yet, and she wasn't sure I cared enough or had her best interests at heart.

The point of telling you this is that there are times when we have to rush into action and act, even if all the foundations of trust aren't there. Clearly, over time, my wife learned I had her true interest at heart, and today we have over 25 years of marriage as proof of that trust.

The system kept me out of politics and instead focused me on demonstrating the foundations of trust. Now, I weave the model of trust into all of my teams—including team "Schmidt and Massey." If I continued to express that I had other's interests ahead of my own, even when trust was in question, then you can do the same. Even if it takes a few years to get the foundations of trust, it can happen.

Marvel at Your Power

Our best friend's daughter has always called me her twin (she's 40+ years younger than me which makes this especially funny). For my birthday, she decided we needed matching Iron Man costumes.

So many thoughts ran through my head. First, *how do I put this on?* Next, *is this going to fit?* And then, *won't I look silly?*

I wore it anyway.

This was Thanksgiving weekend. As we walked through the neighborhood together in our matching costumes, people waved at us, drivers honked, and everyone cheered us on. Of course, they knew I was doing it for her, and they were celebrating us. My fears of looking foolish disappeared.

She said, "We are so much alike, the only way they can tell who is who is by the size of our hands!"

When we were headed home, she asked, "Wasn't this your best day ever?!?"

And it really was; we just had fun.

Because she believed in me as her twin, I realized I could empower her by simply putting her interests ahead of my own. I had to get over my resistance. Why was I so worried about wearing a costume anyway? Nobody cared! I was putting all these obstacles in the way to prevent myself from giving my "twin" a great day, and it turned out to be a remarkable day for me too.

This experience reminded me of some valuable lessons. Never be afraid to tell others what their superpower is, and never be afraid to accept the powers others see in you. Accept your power. Accept you can. And help others to do the same.

By now we should all understand what trust is, but the question is, how do we apply it? And that question is answered when you find your 'I' and identify your purpose. Trust in action takes shape when foundational trust at the self, team, and system level, meets action.

Foundational trust plus action is . . . trust in action.

6

The Value *of* Values

Culture eats strategy for breakfast. What I mean by that is that culture is how things get done.

In the early 2000's, after our company was acquired by AstraZeneca, I was asked to be part of a three-day workshop centered around company values. It was called something along the lines of "Culture Jam," and, though I questioned the cheesy name and having an uncool middle aged white guy as one of the hosts for the activity, it worked. The most interesting thing that came out of this workshop was that we started crowdsourcing our company values.

Once we had narrowed it down to a few values, the employees were asked to provide some behaviors they felt represented those values. What followed was the fastest shift in cultural change I'd ever seen, and the employees witnessed it in real time. By defining those values rooted in social purpose, discovering the reason for our company's existence, and allowing employees to provide their input, we galvanized our company culture.

As this cultural shift was taking place around the company, I was asked to lead the team responsible for building the compliance program for the North American division of AstraZeneca. This was a division that had been in back-to-back Corporate Integrity Agreements with the U.S. government for alleged unethical marketing and sales practices. When I joined their compliance team, I noticed right away that there was a general philosophy from many of my compliance colleagues that the commercial employees couldn't be trusted and that we had to spell every rule out to the lowest denominator.

I came in with no assumptions, yet, as a self-identified five-and-dime behaviorist, I was shocked. Instead of finding the root cause of the issues, my colleagues generated more policies and more rules. We created a cottage industry of investigating people for violating internal policies and rules. For instance, there were more than ten meal limits that our sales people were asked to follow. Every time a rep went above his or her meal limit, my team had to investigate, regardless of the amount. Sometimes it was only a nominal amount over the per person limit, which was easy to do if one person who RSVP'd didn't show up. Regardless, members of Compliance would have to investigate and document the extent of the meal limit violation. It was arbitrary and ridiculous; a third of my investigations were minor breaches.

Finally, I just said enough. *What are we trying to accomplish with all these meal limits?*

What it boiled down to for me was that this was a business budget issue, not a compliance issue. I set a fixed dollar limit for any meal at any given time. We changed the controls and simplified the process. This simplification transformed our program into a principles-based culture instead of a rule-focused culture. If you didn't know how to act—or in this case, how much to spend—you had to exercise judgment. We removed the artificial security blanket that rules provide. From now on, employees would have to use independent judgment and accountability and work with line managers to make the right business decisions.

Constantly asking for permission doesn't foster a culture of innovation or trust.

After the success of overhauling the U.S. policy program, I was asked to take over the global, enterprise-wide program. One night, I found myself sitting in front of my computer screen with a 30-page code of conduct manual open on my desktop. I felt the same despair I felt when discovering all the red tape surrounding the former meal plan regime.

I wondered, *how am I going to simplify this?*

I pride myself on being an innovator. I pride myself on using thinking that is different from the thinking that caused the problems. As I was reading an open letter from our former CEO, I noticed a line that said, "Our code of conduct sets our company values and the behaviors expected of all the employees around the world."

Then it hit me. The letter said it all. A code outlines the values and behaviors expected for all employees around the world.

I remembered our "Culture Jam" and the refresh of our company values. We'd nailed it down to five values and two behaviors for each value, and we already had more than half of our employees around the world actively engaged and bought into the idea. We retired our old code of conduct manual and replaced it with five values and ten behaviors. It wasn't 30 pages of laws and risks; it was a one-page document with values we all agreed reflected who we were and what should guide our actions. That way, if an employee was uncertain of how to act, they could easily go down the list of values we co-created and judge for themselves. Instead of "our law review" being the focus of our code, our values would define the behaviors expected of our employees.

Ironically, because a few on the compliance team felt the company couldn't correct the behavior of employees, they tried to control them instead. With a few people controlling many, it snowballed out of control. Compliance churned out rule after rule and meal limit after meal limit, setting employees up for failure by using a stick instead of a carrot. It was overwhelming. Employees were experiencing decision fatigue.

To date, the organization has not had significant violations of behavior since releasing the simplified code of conduct. The organization continues to have ethical business results and even started being recognized as one of the most sustainable companies on the planet. I was invited to appear on the speaker's circuit and was recognized as one of the top minds in this space. That empowerment of our workforce through values-driven behavior transformed our ways of working from compliance and policies to ethical decision making and sustainable, long-term thinking.

Even after I left, our values continued to put out great work in this area, including a no profit, no loss, vaccine and one of the most aggressive climate plans in the world. And it all started with a "Culture Jam" where people were asked to speak up.

This is how you use values to create a culture that drives processes, practices, structures, and governance of a company. Yes, our values need to be centered around what matters, but the values must also drive a culture that allows things to get done.

The value of values is that they are the source of culture and ultimately performance. Values can be social norms and standards or part of the lexicon and actions that employees take on day to day. When tackling complex situations, employees can always come back to values to inform their behavior and decisions.

In short, value drives behavior, which drives culture.

Buzzworthy Values

Recently, researchers conducted a study to discover which core values were the most popular amongst the Fortune 500 companies. They evaluated 2,057 values gathered from a total of 397 organizations including Amazon, Apple, and Microsoft. The end result was five values that were seen consistently across all the companies: integrity, teamwork, innovation, customer service, and respect.

That's not surprising because I've seen these values everywhere.

What this tells me is that companies are just taking on corporate buzz words like "integrity" and "teamwork," but these aren't their true values. Take Enron for example, which un-ironically had the word "integrity" emblazoned on the wall of their lobby. One of the things companies struggle with today is how to differentiate themselves from cookie-cutter corporate values that don't translate into behaviors. How do we drive a culture that isn't just one-size-fits-all?

The value of values isn't just words in a lobby or meaningless data points. Real values drive culture, shape policy, and transform companies. If you are aligned with why you exist, your values should be clear and unique.

At Zai Labs, for instance, when the CEO Samantha Du was building the enterprise she wanted to lead, she was looking to create a culture based on values right from the start. When they talk about gender equity as one of our values, they actually have gender equity. Not just in leadership and base pay, but they have women in P&L and in STEM positions. Their data aren't just window dressing so they can say they have a certain percentage of women in leadership. They have gender equity built into the core aspects of the business itself.

That's the difference when you create a culture of values that takes into account everything they know from all the mistakes and the learnings of the past—both the positive and the negative.

Culture At our Core

There are many who say companies can't and shouldn't have human values.

I couldn't disagree more.

Business is one of the built systems we as humans create to construct order in our world. Therefore, it is very reasonable to expect humanity at work. Cultures authentically grounded in strong values and focused on the personal care and support of others are inspiring, enlightening, and transformational. They also produce extraordinary business results.

When I enter my workplace, I have to accept that I'm not here for what Jim Massey wants; I'm here to advance the interests of the company. I need to reconcile my own personal values with the company's values and decide whether they align enough to justify me working there (which is why I won't work for some industries).

When I join companies, I want them to value human rights over control of humans. That means there will be differences and conflict. In my line of work, it is not uncommon for me to encounter people I disagree with. I have met climate change deniers while trying to advance a climate agenda. Climate change is one of the most contentious subjects on the planet. My response has always been, "I respect your perspective. Yet, based on company values, this is the company's position. Luckily, we have many programs across many topics. If you don't agree with our environmental program, please find how you can help drive other initiatives."

The direction was clear, but the response from employees was mixed. Often, employees would move on to other topics. In some circumstances, I would need to speak with employees 1:1 to help them realize the company position further and help them find where they could contribute.

Having the company value of inclusion means that

employees will have individual values that don't necessarily align perfectly across the board. Through managing conflict effectively, we can drive innovation and wake people up to their true purpose instead of rewarding sleepwalkers mindlessly going through the motions at work each day.

There are three rules of thumb to remember when it comes to values. One, speak about your values often. Have some process in place for sharing your core values with others, which includes clear reasoning and why they matter. Two, actually live out these values. If your core values don't align with why you exist and your purpose, and if that doesn't mean something to the organization, none of this will work. If your employees see you violating a core value or your colleagues and management team don't abide by those values, your culture is in trouble. Three, hold companies accountable for their values. This involves having tough conversations with people and having a regular gut check on the core values of your organization.

When I talk about corporate values, I'm not implying that a company must have a full list. As with everything in life, a business must prioritize what values are non-negotiable and define what behaviors are acceptable with variances. A company shouldn't be trying to outline every behavior expected of every employee 24/7. We're never going to be able to create an ideal corporate 'sandbox' where nobody ever throws sand. Instead of trying to control humans, we should be allowing real people to drive culture around the values of decency, dignity, and respect.

I recently came across an article that cited a SHRM poll of over 1,500 HR professionals and found only 8 percent of organizations had communicated guidelines to employees around political discussions at work. The authors of the article bemoaned this fact as the U.S. heads into the contentious 2022 midterm elections.

Why are we still dictating guidelines for things like conversation and dress code? Moreover, why do we still have HR departments with the sole purpose of managing people? We're so beyond that now.

Everyone says they want an inclusive culture and sustainability, but our HR departments and so-called best practices were built for companies that weren't inclusive or sustainable to begin with. The very metrics we use to evaluate companies were created in a vastly different landscape of cultural values. It's time to move beyond that. We aren't going to solve the problems of today by using the same thinking that got us here.

We are facing existential issues. Petty rules and guidelines aren't going to cut it. We need to value values more than we value control and find ways to drive a culture that aligns with why we exist. We aren't looking for one-size-fits-all. We are looking to define our non-negotiables, and still leave plenty of room for employees to feel comfortable being themselves and offering fresh solutions. When we do this well, the culture is clear, but so too is our commitment to care about others. Now that we know we can, in the next section, we will discuss how we show we care.

PART 2
CARE

7

Show Me More

Growing up in Missouri, our state motto was "show me." I've always had a belief that if you can't show me, then you don't care.

Many companies are still struggling with this concept, which was painfully evident by the mass exodus of employees from the workplace during and after the COVID-19 global pandemic. A shocking amount of people resigned, quit, or shifted to working remotely between 2020 and 2022, and this trend shows no signs of slowing. The other day, I came across a statistic[3] from a survey that found a staggering one in five workers globally

---

3 https://www.weforum.org/agenda/2022/06/the-great-resignation-is-not-over/

plans on quitting their job in 2022. Employee burnout has permeated companies, even among executives. A recent Deloitte survey[4] found that 69% of C-suite executives said they were "seriously considering quitting for a job that better supports their well-being."

This phenomenon has been dubbed "quiet quitting" or the "Great Resignation," and companies are scrambling to figure out the needs of their employees—and, more importantly, how to meet them.

While most of the people they surveyed said money was the motivating factor for switching employers, many of them also said finding fulfilling work and the opportunity to be one's authentic self at work was part of the equation. This tells me that employees are no longer satisfied with working for companies that are so focused on making quarterly returns, they're forgetting the social impact and human aspect of work. In other words, employees are not convinced these companies *care*.

Workers are saying, "Show me you care."

Stakeholder Capitalism

In today's business environment, if companies want to retain their employees, they're going to have to do more than just offer them a raise. The largest generation in the workforce today, Millennials[5], are overwhelmingly looking to join companies that

---

4 https://nypost.com/2022/06/22/many-c-suite-executives-want-to-quit-over-burnout-survey/

5 https://www.greatplacetowork.com/press-releases/2021-fortune-best-workplaces-for-millennials-press-release

offer equity, transparency, and purpose. Employees are looking for ethical companies that value them and try to do good. On the flip side, consumers are looking for companies that make a positive impact and, at a minimum, are not doing harm to people and the planet.

We can no longer afford to focus solely on quarterly returns and investors. For quite some time, shareholders ruled. Yet, the evidence is clear. We need to transition from worrying solely about our investors and how business operations are affecting money to worrying about how we're impacting our planet and people—employees, customers, partners, supply chains, and communities.

Today, the idea is that if we take care of customers, employees, and our communities, our business will be successful and generate shareholder value. Leaders must constantly balance the input they are receiving from the people who are impacted by the business with what matters most to the business itself.

This is stakeholder capitalism 101, the current era of business.

Who Cares Wins

In 2000, the U.N. Global Compact was formed. Four years later, a report came out titled "Who Cares Wins: Connecting Financial Markets to a Changing World," and the term ESG was coined. Today ESG needs no introduction, but this framework that was originally meant as a way to communicate what you do and why to investors has been repositioned.

I have seen ESG go mainstream and serve as the backbone for stakeholder capitalism.

Stakeholder capitalism aims to create returns for investors by creating more value for all stakeholders: from employees to customers, supply chains, distribution partners, communities, and the planet. It covers everything from lobbying and influencing regulations to business operations and product impact—all the material topics for what matters to your customers, employees, and to the business itself.

Because stakeholder capitalism encompasses so much, trust is more important than ever. It is paramount. Stakeholders must see how companies care if they are to trust the organization. Ultimately, I see the future of ESG boiling down to trust.

Companies should serve their shareholders as well as societal interests, and the two can be mutually beneficial when done right. It's not just about what you can do for your shareholders, but your ability to demonstrate that there is a shared benefit for everyone impacted by your organization.

Whether you call it ESG, stakeholder capitalism, or simply trust, the complexities of balancing stakeholder needs with business priorities is still an ongoing discussion in many industries. There is a complexity to engaging the right internal and external stakeholders with the right topics. Priority and alignment are key.

Ruffling Feathers

Change is hard. It doesn't happen easily, but accepting the status quo will not create the immediate systemic change we need to tackle some of our biggest issues. In 2021, the United Nations

Secretary-General indicated the world is "tremendously off track" to achieving the Sustainable Development Goals (SDGs) by 2030. I continue to see our global systems working to protect and benefit a few instead of the global population. This will only change when all of us are equally uncomfortable.

I can't tell you how many times I have heard so-called business experts advising investors, executives, and managers not to take a stance on political topics at work. This has always been curious to me, as companies are trying to address key topics like climate change and DEI. Personally, I talk about racial injustice and other ESG topics because these things matter a great deal to my colleagues and to me. People and planet are interconnected, and I have a moral obligation to give a voice to those who cannot speak up. Doing otherwise upholds the old acronym "BAU" (meaning business as usual) instead of the new mantra I use, business as us. We must create cultures where human beings are relevant and valued.

One time, I was doing a training for various board members and one of my co-presenters said, "We need to make sure that companies don't take a stance on political topics."

Me being me, I said, "What do you consider political topics?"

"Like race," he said. I waited to see if any of the other people trained on ESG were going to speak up, and they didn't. (Most of them were white, if you hadn't guessed.) We were training directors on ESG, which was a hot topic at the time. Without any other attendees saying anything, I had to speak up. Though we were a relatively homogeneous group, I am driven by the need to care, even when those I'm caring about aren't in the room.

Five months into the COVID-19 pandemic and just a few months after the murder of George Floyd, I was in between jobs and was invited to be part of a cohort training to make the most of our LinkedIn profiles. The expert was talking about various topics and said, "It is important to remember LinkedIn isn't supposed to be political."

Again, I had to ask what he meant by political. His response was very similar to the earlier example.

"So, if you want to tread lightly, you can talk about mask wearing, and I would stay away from race related topics."

Again, the audience was predominantly white, and again, I waited curiously to see how others would respond. When no one spoke, I said, "I need to offer a different perspective. I'm not comfortable with your suggestion to stay away from racial issues on LinkedIn, especially in today's environment when companies are actively trying to address DEI and basic human rights."

We continued to discuss the topic, sharing our different views. Ultimately, he said, "We will need to agree to disagree."

And I said, "As a white man, I understand why you'd say that. But I am speaking for those not on this call so that the leaders on the call know that we must step up. Basic human rights are not political, and each of us must do our part to protect them."

On the call, no other leaders provided a perspective either way. However, immediately following the call, I had a third of the participants message me to either share their appreciation of me for saying something or to request a meeting with me to discuss further. Over the course of the next week, I met with most of the participants who reached out, and they told me the major reason they did not speak up is because they were afraid they would say something wrong. They questioned their own capability and knowledge on the topic—they didn't know what to say. In this instance, the lack of trust in their own ability prevented them from taking action.

When you have some of the most powerful influencers in business calling for a shift in priorities—like BlackRock CEO Larry Fink, who recently challenged companies to demonstrate more social responsibility in an open letter[6] to shareholders—you know that companies can no longer sit idly by or avoid topics that matter to society at large. Look how far we've come from 2014, when no company would take a stance on the Black Lives Matter protests, to 2021, when CEOs were actively commenting on the George Floyd murder verdict.

With the emergence of CEO and employee activism, taking a stance on important social and environmental issues is front and center—and it's important for business and leaders to know when to take a stand. We cannot take a stance on every topic. The average company could take on 100 different societal issues, but, in order to build trust as a business, you must prioritize the topics that will be vital to the changes you'd like to make.

I like to say, 'priority isn't meant to be plural.' Science-based companies should focus on STEM; entertainment companies should focus on programming and the arts; schools should focus on education, and so on. If you've truly identified the reason why you exist, it shouldn't be hard to figure out where you can make the most impact and, therefore, understand when your stakeholders need to hear your voice. The past few years

---

6 https://www.blackrock.com/corporate/investor-relations/larry-fink-ceo-letter

have highlighted the role employees play in corporate activism. Employees serve as a wonderful litmus test on societal topics. Companies must take a stand, and, likewise, employees can't be afraid to ruffle feathers or to speak up on topics that matter. In fact, sometimes the best way to get the ball rolling is by ruffling the feathers of an ally or an executive who is on your side and has the power to make changes.

Triple Bottom Line

Every time I attend an investor conference or meet with investors, I always remind them that it's actually the everyday workers—our employees, teachers, and government workers—that supply the funds we are discussing, and these are the same people who are the consumers driving consumption, and thus, the company's profits. These are our stakeholders.

For instance, institutional investors are making decisions for my 401K, and, yes, they're trying to outperform the market, make profit, and get their bonuses, but they are doing so on behalf of the workers and the consumers, the people upon whom the economy is built. Yes, the Wall Street system is disproportionally paying investors astronomical amounts, but, in the end, it's not their money. It's ours. We need to remember this, so we can continue to evolve ESG into a framework to easily communicate, disclose, and evaluate both performance and impact.

Prove to the consumers and employees that you care enough to create products and services that address the issues they face and, in turn, they will become more loyal. The EY's Future

Consumer Index 2022 suggests that 43 percent of consumers want to buy from companies that benefit society and 64 percent are prepared to behave differently if it benefits society. In the end, more loyal and trusting consumers give the investors the returns they want.

Stakeholder capitalism means moving from focusing on quarterly returns to focusing on long term urgent ethical decision making, specifically the "triple bottom line" of people, planet, and profits.

The Future of Trust

After the 2005 Who Cares Wins Conference, organizers issued several key learnings, one of which was that ESG factors should be truly "mainstreamed" and not treated as a separate category. One participant remarked that, "pigeonholing ESG as a separate category will kill it."

Fast forward two decades later, we still see the struggle of taking ESG mainstream. Progress in creating change has been slow and for exactly the reason the same paper identified. Investing in long-term value by integrating environmental, social, and governance value-drivers in asset management and financial research could be suppressed by powerful forces exclusively interested in short-term gains (a majority of institutional investors were seen as behaving this way; hedge funds were mentioned).

Our obsession with quarterly gains continues to drive the lack of focus on what once were long-term issues. Food scarcity, climate change, and human inequalities are now ever present and causing chaos around the world. The time to act is now. A key action we need to take is demonstrating that others' interests matter. As the United Nations initiative in 2004 title stated so eloquently: Who Cares Wins.

8

Humanity *at* Work

When my wife and I had our first child, we had a difficult time conceiving. Anyone who has struggled with fertility knows that IVF treatments are expensive and the process can be heartbreaking and exhausting.

Fortunately, I was working at Johnson & Johnson, and my insurance covered most of the IVF treatment. We ended up only paying a nominal fee. When we welcomed our first child into the world, I also had plenty of time off for parental leave. My wife, on the other hand, was working at another company, and she got the minimum legal requirement. In fact, she ended up using her vacation time, sick days, and some unpaid leave just to have the time she wanted after the baby was born.

Everyone was shocked at the benefits and paternity leave that were offered to us from J & J. To me, this wasn't surprising. Johnson & Johnson is a baby company; it's part of why they exist. They made sure their benefits were spectacular because healthy babies are part of their purpose and something they deeply care about.

Some companies care about *people*, and others don't.

We need to show we care, and the way we do that is through transforming our organizations. Trust in action can be applied to any place where our stakeholders interact with or rely upon our systems. Examining the system through the lens of each stakeholder is the best way to determine how to go about demonstrating that we care.

Workforce

As I write these words, companies are laying off thousands of workers in what looks like the beginning of a post-COVID recession. Nothing will give you a better idea of whether a company cares or not than a layoff.

In his first week of ownership, Elon Musk laid off 3,700 employees after acquiring Twitter in 2022. Workers were sent emails with a subject line that simply said "Your Role at Twitter," notifying them of their termination. In addition, thousands of contractors were let go and remote work was banned, forcing the remaining employees to come into the office or find another job. Elon was very clear: it was about the financials.

Perhaps out of embarrassment or conscience, former CEO Jack Dorsey issued a statement on Twitter on behalf of the company apologizing for growing Twitter too quickly.

Patrick Collins, the CEO of tech company Stripe, published a similar open email on November 3rd, saying that they had over-hired and taking responsibility for the "consequential mistakes" they'd made when scaling the company in a very different economic climate. They had to reduce their employee headcount at Stripe, cutting almost 14 percent of their workforce, but the way they handled it was much more humane, in my opinion.

Stripe graciously offered departing employees 14 weeks of severance pay, healthcare coverage for six months, PTO, bonuses, career counseling, and immigration support. They met with all the departing employees one-on-one; they didn't fire them via email. More importantly, the executives took the names of those who were being laid off and sent them to people they knew in the tech industry to help the former employees find work. To me, they demonstrated that they actually cared about their people.

If you don't respect your employees or care about people, how do you think your organization is going to continue to operate? That's my question.

If I were an employee, I would look carefully at how the CEOs handle layoffs before joining a company. Likewise, businesses should understand that this is a key area where they can demonstrate they truly care about their workforce.

Consumer

As I've mentioned earlier, there are some model companies that are doing a great job of having consumer interests at heart. We already mentioned Southwest Airlines, but some of my personal favorites include All Birds, Bomba Socks, and Tom's.

These companies are searching their supply chains from source to shelves looking for holistic solutions and discovering ways in which they can source the goods for the products they make without taking away from our planet. The reason they're doing this is because they care about natural resources, but they also understand that this is something their consumers care about.

One thing these companies all have in common is that they offer their customers a "do-good" incentive. They're rethinking their model of manufacturing and sourcing in a way that allows the customer to feel that, when they buy a product, they aren't just feeding unnecessary consumption; they're actually making an impact on someone else's life.

This is an important area where showing that you care about more than just profits can actually make or break your brand. These companies are doing it right.

Supply Chain

In our neighborhood, Tony's chocolate bars are the go-to for kids' parties. Not just because of their bright colorful wrappers and delicious chocolate, but because of their work to end modern slavery, including child labor.

Tony's Chocolonely has launched a mission to make chocolate supply chains 100% slave free. Even though they've never found an instance of slave labor in their supply chain, they can't guarantee that modern day chocolate sources are slave free. Illegal labor exists, especially in regions without schools where it is legal for children as young as 14 years old to work. That's why it's important to raise the standards in the multiple systems we operate in.

Tony's is aiming to change the entire process surrounding cacao sourcing, but we don't want Tony's building schools. The people who make chocolate bars shouldn't be setting standards for education in West Africa. That isn't their expertise. What they can do is focus on safe and ethical working environments and provide fair living wages to farmers so that families don't have to send their children into the workforce.

There are many ways companies can show that they care about people. The best ways that they can do this is by being sincere in their purpose, focusing on the area they can make the most impact, and treating the people who are impacted by their business with consideration. Companies, and especially the leaders who run them, have the ethical obligation to empower their workforces, including supply chain workers, as all industries evolve from the current state to the future state of business.

As a leader what is your responsibility?

Within your operational ecosystem, it is your workforce, your consumers, and your supply chain. Externally, it is your investors, regulators, and government. Now that we've covered the systems that businesses deal with operationally, let's move to the greater systems outside of day-to-day operations.

Unlike the previous examples we just discussed, these external systems are tricky. We often hear about bad actors and very seldomly about good actors.

Investors

Balancing all stakeholders is not an easy task. Especially when we are stuck between the space of quarterly returns and long-term impact. The two don't naturally align. The pressure to deliver quarter on quarter can easily block our long view of progress, until something sneaks up because we didn't have our sights on the horizon.

Take the recent example of the FTX collapse in the crypto market. CEO Sam Bankman-Fried borrowed money from FTX's balance sheet for investments which bankrupted his investors. Many lost their life savings in his investment scheme. When asked in interviews about his intentions and whether or not he knowingly did wrong, he just said, "It wasn't my intention. Life creeps up on you."

My guess from reading his comments, his disdain for regulators, the way he disparages ESG, is that he never had his investors' best interests at heart. His cavalier attitude towards the people who were impacted by his shortsighted mistakes tells me he wasn't interested in benefiting anyone but himself in the short term.

We are seeing this in the public sector as well. Individual politics trump the financial well-being of the investors themselves. Leaders are choosing their agenda over what is best for those they govern or lead. If they truly cared, they would want to maximize the returns and minimize the fees for the investors in their states. We will get into that more in a bit, but first let's talk about regulators.

Regulators

When we engage with regulators, the general expectation is that business just needs to 'do it.' Companies have money and can adjust to anything that is required. However, it is not always that easy, and often business only meets the letter of the law, but not the *spirit* of the law.

Case in point, the SEC's CEO pay ratio disclosure requirement. Starting in 2018, public companies must annually disclose the ratio of the median total compensation of their employees (other than the Chief Executive Officer) and the annual total compensation of their Chief Executive Officer.

The SEC mandated pay disclosure[7] in hopes that it would correct discrepancies. As of this writing, it has not. Businesses just met the bare minimum of disclosure without addressing the desired outcome of pay equity and alignment.

Even with the disclosure, the average S&P 500 executive salary has climbed by about $500,000 a year for ten straight years, while average worker wages have increased by just $1,303, topping out at $58,260 in 2021.

Interestingly, regulators continue to drive change in pay, primarily focused on the transparency of pay. In 2022, 17 states

---

7 https://www.bloomberg.com/news/newsletters/2022-11-08/salary-transparency-has-some-unintended-consequences

have pay transparency laws, the most progressive of which requires employers to provide salary ranges in job postings. Recent actions include pay transparency in job postings.

The CEO of Gravity Payments Dan Price made headlines when he stopped taking pay in order to increase his workers' salaries. He set a groundbreaking $70,000 yearly minimum wage for his employees. The problem was all his efforts were tarnished when he was accused of sexual harassment at his company and was forced to resign.

This is one of the biggest struggles in corporate America. When an organization does one thing right, it does something else wrong, and people ignore the good because of the bad. We have to stop that. Obviously, I'm not condoning the behavior of this CEO, but his way of showing that he cares about his stakeholders at the salary level can and should be replicated by others.

People Over Politics

With the unfortunate politicization of ESG in the U.S. right now, several states are waging war against what they call 'woke capitalism.'

Florida governor Ron DeSantis has publicly stated that the state's pension funds will not be considering ESG criteria when seeking to generate returns. Banning businesses and banks from public pensions is putting politics over people.

While it's well within a governor's rights to tell BlackRock, "not in my state," going to smaller asset managers with higher fees will have some financial repercussions. Blocking portfolios from accessing retirement funds that are tainted with 'woke

ESG capital' mainly hurts the investors, the government workers, teachers, and state pension employees.

Despite this war being waged against ESG, I strongly believe that government can work with business, and vice versa, to get things done. The way we do that is by influencing policies and improving decision making overall. For instance, President Biden recently announced[8] that the largest purchasing organization in the world—the U.S. government—would require anyone in its supply chain to disclose their environmental impacts through CDP and to make good on their promises by setting science-based targets.

By doing this, the government is showing the citizens that it cares about them as well as the planet. In turn, this should drive more trust in the systems the government creates.

It is important to clarify that I do support companies making money, but I balance this idea with a common catch phrase in the sustainability field: "You can't do business on a dead planet."

You may get great quarterly returns for five years, but climate change can wipe all that out in a second. This is why leaders need to understand the human and planetary impact of caring. The next chapter is focused on our biggest stakeholder: the planet.

---

8 https://www.cdp.net/en/articles/media/in-bold-new-move-biden-administration-makes-cdps-model-the-law

9
What *on* Earth?

When I was in third grade, as part of the Missouri Arbor Day celebration, every student received a sapling to plant. I planted an ash sapling that grew to a thirty-foot tall tree, and it still stands on the family farm today. It survived forty winters, countless dry and wet spells, and even a close call with a tree disease. I've always been proud of that one resilient tree.

The thought of that ash tree always helps motivate me when I feel overwhelmed with the environmental crisis we face today. There's a saying, "He who believes in something plants a tree."

I learned early on the importance of believing in something and of planting a tree, but I had no idea that decades later this tree would become transformative in my own leadership journey at AstraZeneca.

Planting the Seed

One day, I got tagged in a post from a Bulgarian colleague who knew our electric vehicle program wouldn't get to her region for another five years. Instead of waiting to make an impact, she decided to plant a tree instead. She challenged a few of us leaders to join her in planting a tree as part of a program she called the AZ Forest. As a leader in sustainability and as a fellow tree enthusiast, I engaged and so did more than 38,000 employees. Within one year, colleagues around the world planted more than 70,000 trees on the six continents on which we operated.

This program inspired me as I was creating our industry-leading environmental program, Ambition Net Zero. As we designed and delivered one of the world's first net zero programs, we also drove home the importance of net positive biodiversity programs. The biggest challenge we had was finding the right global partner. Luckily, when I put out a request for proposals, One Tree Planted stood out as the right organization to help with one of the biggest programs we could take on as a company.

From this partnership, we developed and scaled one of the most progressive environmental programs centered around reforestation at AstraZeneca to date. By the time we went live with our numbers, we'd committed to plant 50 million trees by 2025. That one tree planted in Bulgaria became a groundbreaking 50 million trees—all because one person decided, *hey, I can plant a tree and make a difference.*

This became an integral part of our transformative initiatives at AstraZeneca. By allowing nature to do what it does best—absorb carbon—this program also helped establish one of the most robust environmental programs in the industry. We didn't take any offsets; we were just doing good. One person and one tree were all it took to challenge me to transform as a leader.

Nature and Nurture

When we talk about our development as humans, we often try to decide how much we attribute to nature or nurture. When I think about the development of organizations and why they need to care about our planet, it has to be both. It's nature and nurture. The earth is our "nature." But we also need to think about our built systems and how what we create is harming, hurting, or depleting the planet.

What applies to us as humans can also be applied to the planet itself. When nature is being harmed or it isn't being nurtured, we need to take both "nature and nature" into account, because this planet is our HOME, and the earth is our greatest asset.

Assets Not Offsets

According to Bloomberg Business, housing represents 63 percent of the total wealth held by most Americans. Throughout business school, I was always reminded to focus on buying a home because it would become my biggest asset. Most leaders with whom I speak generally agree with this idea; they understand the importance of property management both personally and professionally. Yet when it comes to the collective of humanity, we seem to lose sight of our shared greater asset that needs protecting: our home, Earth.

U.N. Secretary General António Guterres told ministers of 40 countries attending the July 2022 Petersberg Climate Dialogue that, "We have a choice. Collective action or collective suicide. It is in our hands."

In 2022, the United Nations General Assembly recognized that everyone everywhere has the right to live in a clean, healthy, and sustainable environment. For those in power, respecting this right is no longer an option but an obligation. Although not legally binding, the U.N. resolution is expected to accelerate action, just as earlier resolutions on the right to water in 2010 turbocharged progress in delivering safe water to millions of people.

Everyone is so focused on climate and greenhouse gas emissions that we rarely hear about an equally important crisis: biodiversity. Together with the goal of net-zero emissions by 2050, the U.N. has set the goal of net positive biodiversity by 2030. We need to go beyond conservation in order to achieve this goal; we will need a breakthrough in how we produce, consume, and govern over the next eight years.

At the start of 2020, this decade was deemed the decade of our lives. We are currently 20 percent through this decade and we are still not on track to meet any of the targets or indicators of the SDGs. In 2013, it was estimated that we would need 1.7 planets to make humanity's consumption sustainable. We don't have that; there is just one Earth.

Another way to look at how quickly we are using our natural resources is through the Earth Overshoot Day calculated by the Global Footprint Network. To determine the date of Earth Overshoot Day for each year, Global Footprint Network calculates the number of days of that year that Earth's biocapacity suffices to provide for humanity's Ecological Footprint. The remainder of the year corresponds to global overshoot. Earth Overshoot Day is computed by dividing the planet's biocapacity (the amount of ecological resources Earth is able to generate that year), by humanity's Ecological Footprint (humanity's demand for that year), and multiplying by 365, the number of days in a year. (Planet's Biocapacity/Humanity's Ecological Footprint × 365 = Earth Overshoot Day.)

In 2022, the Earth Overshoot Day was July 28, one of the earliest dates calculated.

Nature has become a commodity for us to use. As a result, we now live on an angry and hot planet, and nature has begun to lash out in ways that could be potentially catastrophic for civilization. We need a shift from thinking of our impact on the planet in terms of offsets to guarding this precious asset that we all share. As pioneers in this movement, we can create a new asset class based on nature and its benefits—the ecosystem services—we gain from the earth.

Companies would be wise to make this shift. Some businesses, on the other hand, have it right from the start.

All it Takes is One

Patagonia is a stellar example of a business that treats the planet like an asset. The founder, Yvon Chouinard, was an avid mountain climber, and, from this love of climbing, he decided to help the world enjoy the sport. Chouinard's company always had a purpose, which was focused on enjoying the outdoors responsibly and celebrating the earth. As a result, Patagonia's products and culture were always rooted in its cause. Patagonia clothing and gear may be expensive, but they reclaim clothes, have a specific department devoted to fixing clothing, and often reuse materials.

Recently, Patagonia's founder announced he is choosing to forgo all profit and any tax benefits and is donating these funds to a foundation focused on climate change initiatives. Chouinard's statement was simple: "I never want to be beholden to investors, and now we have just one: earth."

This is an excellent example of trust in action, as well as treating the planet as a precious asset.

From a recent interview with Chouinard:

> "Chouinard's choice to forgo the profit of a sale or even the tax benefits of organizing the transfer through a charity 'raises questions that should be discussed in every boardroom,'" shares Aron Cramer. "'What is our purpose? What are we trying to accomplish? Are we making good on our aspirations on social, economic, and environmental matters?'"

This man believed in appreciating nature so strongly that he created a successful business around it, and then decided the only thing he cared about was saving the planet. That is the spirit we want to bring into all our business dealings and built systems, and it can be done, but only if we are willing to genuinely transform our operations.

Another company I admire in the space is Unilever. They're clearly a leader in sustainability according to today's standards. Even though Unilever has made significant steps towards its stated goal, a leading organization like this is trapped in trying to *improve* instead of disrupt and transform its business operations. My goal with this book is to try and help leaders in organizations develop the self-awareness to say, "Hey, we still aren't addressing the core business operations most negatively impacting the planet," and focus their efforts where they can have the greatest impact.

Unilever has an opportunity to do just this. As of December 2022, the company had this statement posted on its company website:

> "Our ambition is to make sustainable and deforestation-free palm oil commonplace and to only source from low-risk locations. To achieve this, we're stepping up our engagement with suppliers and small holders while increasing the traceability and transparency of our supply chain."

Palm oil is found in more than half of the packaged products Americans use, including ice cream, lipstick, soaps, and detergents, according to the World Wildlife Fund. Farmers in developing nations are burning rainforests to make way for palm oil plantations, removing a vital carbon sink and reducing biodiversity in the process. So even though some practices may be certified, the process involved is speeding up the issues we are trying to fix.

Instead of fixing the old broken system and labeling this

10

Stepping Into *the* B.S.

We operate in what I call the built systems, which I lovingly refer to as B.S. for short—the spaces humans create to bring order to our chaos. These systems are our government and religious institutions, media, educational systems, industries, businesses, and communities. Within the systems, we have laws, regulations, and industry standards that we all must follow. These built systems exist all around us and impact us daily. For example, within a business system, a company has its code of conduct for employees, an educational system provides the industry's standardized testing benchmark, or a government system establishes environmental policies.

A day doesn't go by that we don't hear about climate change, human rights oppressions, threats of geo-political unrest, gender and race inequities, or the failures of government leaders being discussed in the news and on social media. The constant 24-hours of information overload is the white noise of the B.S. (built systems) we face daily.

We are living in polarizing times, and some days the "B.S." is too much. Just as we struggle to make sense of a world full of uncertainty and show others we can and care, so do corporations, governments, and institutions. The interplay between individuals and the built systems becomes more complex as we come under increasing pressure to act on behalf of humanity and our planet.

Brought to You by Greenwashing

Corporate sponsorships have long been a way companies leverage their can and care, but in today's business arena, that is not enough. Consumers, employees, and other stakeholders are expecting organizations and leaders to walk the walk, take action, and simply do. Business is one of the only remaining systems where society still places trust, but even that trust is fragile.

For instance, outrage was sparked when it was discovered that the "world's top plastic polluter" Coca-Cola was sponsoring COP27, the yearly U.N. climate meeting being held in Egypt. The soft drink company was accused of "greenwashing."[10] Many

---

10 https://www.theguardian.com/environment/2022/oct/04/cop27-climate-summit-sponsorship-polluter-coca-cola-condemned-as-greenwash

saw this move as a dishonest attempt to hijack the green movement for PR opportunities in lieu of making any real changes to their operations.

Coca-Cola issued a statement saying, "We are prepared to do our part and have set ambitious goals for our business, starting with helping to collect and recycle a bottle or can for every one we sell—regardless of where it comes from—by 2030. In 2020 we signed a joint statement urging United Nations member states to adopt a global treaty to tackle the plastic waste issue through a holistic, circular economy approach . . . Our support for COP27[11] is in line with our science-based target to reduce absolute carbon emissions 25% by 2030, and our ambition for net zero carbon emissions by 2050."

Keep in mind, Coca-Cola has a long history of making impressive sounding commitments and failing to deliver.[12] In the late 90s, Coca-Cola set a target of using 25 percent recycled content in their products by 2015, but thirty years later, that number is still at ten percent.

COP27 was asked to drop Coca-Cola as a sponsor, but in the end, Coca-Cola remained, though they did not participate in the meeting. While individuals at large may not have been able to influence Coca-Cola to put its money where its mouth is this time, we hope that individuals *inside* and outside of Coca-Cola will hold their leaders accountable for fulfilling their commitments to do good.

---

11 https://www.theguardian.com/environment/cop27

12 https://talking-trash.com/case-study/going-round-in-circles-coca-colas-trail-of-broken-promises/#:~:text=In%20the%201990s%2C%20Coca%2DCola,figure%20is%20still%20only%2010%25.

Trust in Action

Organizations have traditionally focused on two elements of trust (can and care) through commitments, long-term targets, and ever evolving concepts of doing good, such as corporate social responsibility, sustainability, and ESG. But time and time again, we see corporations, industries, and global systems like COP convening the greatest minds, sharing promises of transformation, and in the end, as the target dates near, we see little to no meaningful progress.

As I've said before, humans built these systems, and we can change any and all elements required to have the impact desired, if those in charge are willing to deliver all three elements of trust.

As I navigated my career, I developed the model of trust focused on the three core elements: can, care, do. For trust to fall into place, each element must be present. It is possible for any one of the elements to be at play to begin building trust. However, trust won't exist until all three elements are demonstrated through action.

The element of trust that puts trust in action is the third and final element: Do.

A friend once asked me why I am not afraid to take action. Well, I've always had faith that I could. Throughout this book, I've highlighted examples of how I've had to transform so I can lead my teams to change the systems. Why do I continue to transform? Partly because I believe I've been born into the right systems and know I can change those systems built to benefit me. But it also comes down to faith.

Trusting yourself requires faith in your ability to figure out what is needed in an uncertain tomorrow.

11

This I Know

I was never sent to the principal's office. I did, however, get asked to leave my Sunday school class.

I grew up in a Southern Baptist church. It was the spring of 1985 and we were preparing for Easter. My Sunday school teacher, who was also my public school teacher, read us one of the Gospels. She shared that women were the first to see the empty tomb and the first people Jesus encountered after his death. According to scripture, the disciples, all men, didn't believe the women and would not believe these women until they saw for themselves.

This is where I raised my hand. I asked, "Why didn't the men believe the women?"

The response I got was that women couldn't be trusted, and they weren't respected, especially in the context of religion. I wasn't satisfied with that. Instead of accepting the answer and moving on, my next response was, "Well that sounds like an issue for the men, not the women. Jesus decided to come back to women first. Why not trust him?"

My teacher asked me to be quiet and listen.

That was the way it was and still is today. Our church believed men were the spiritual leaders, not women. Still not accepting this as an explanation that made sense, I continued to challenge the unfairness of the matter.

Frustrated with being unable to complete the lesson and move onto the next activity, I was sternly told to sit down and listen to the word of God or go find my parents and ask them to explain. So, I did as I was told. I went and found my parents and asked them the same questions. Lucky for me, I had parents that encouraged me to continue asking questions, grow in my faith, and fight for fairness—no matter what situation or system was trying to correct or control me. I never returned to that Sunday school class again.

I tell this story for two reasons. One, it is one of my earliest examples of realizing how built systems are created to make sense out of the chaos as well as control human behavior. This experience began to shape how I would cover my right-brain dominant creativity. It is one of the first times I remember starting to adjust my ability to "collect dots". I was told to go along to get along; the system worked as designed.

Secondly, I also started to hide my faith around this time, an important part of my identity, to fit into the patriarchal stance of my church. Though I questioned and didn't agree, I learned at the age of ten not to cause a fuss. The system was bigger and stronger and could not be changed.

Oh, I had so much more to learn.

Faith is a Verb

As we've seen, systems can be changed, and we can be transformed by systems, as long as we continue to ask questions, remain open, and trust ourselves. There is a fine line between trust and faith.

When you google faith in 2022, the first definition Google provides is a noun: complete trust or confidence in someone or something.

I see faith as a verb.

As I was preparing to write this book, I was meeting with a dear friend and mentor in the U.K. As usual, he asked a simple, hard-hitting question: why do I trust myself? Why do I trust in action?

My response was immediate and emotional. My faith is why I trust.

Sometimes the B.S. can be too much. When I get overwhelmed or can't find my footing to take the next steps, I turn to my faith as a motivator for action. Faith for me falls into three buckets.

1. **Faith in something larger than us.** I have faith in that which connects us, the system of systems. I also have faith in our "six-degrees of Kevin Bacon" which naturally connects us to one another.

2. **Faith in humanity.** I have faith in people and in the human spirit. I believe in the unmet potential of each of us. At our core, I believe we are good.
3. **Faith in tomorrow.** I believe we have a fresh start and that it goes beyond my next sunrise. I have hope for something better.

How does my faith impact my leadership?

It is what allows me to take action when there is no guarantee, even when I'm faced with issues so large they can be overwhelming. The world doesn't always feel sustainable. Bluntly, most headlines highlight systems full of ugliness, brutal injustices, and expanding inequalities. Yet, at the self and team levels, I see kindness, concern for the future, and the best of humanity at work. Faith allows me to step into the B.S. with confidence.

But I wasn't always this way.

Over the course of my career, I often found myself in spaces and built systems where I felt like I had to hide my Christianity. To some, Christianity represents all the things we dislike about the world around us, but especially division and exclusion. Christianity is a dominant system, especially in the Western world, and yet, because of the stigma surrounding religion, I felt myself concealing it. Over the years, I have met many inclusive, intelligent, loving, and diverse people of all faiths, including Christians, Jews, and Muslims. There is an argument to be made about the many good and bad things about religion—but that is a deeper topic, perhaps for a later book. The point is that I felt it necessary to come out as a Christian because it's fundamental to my leadership and hiding it would be dishonest. It's the guiding light that keeps me going because I have a larger faith in why I'm doing things. I don't expect anyone else to share this moral responsibility, of course. This was solely a step I needed to take in my journey.

All religions are rooted in faith, and all faiths are about connecting to something larger, as well as those around you. We are at a point in our society where the benefits of sharing your faith with others, even at work, are undeniable. David Miller[13], director of the Princeton University Faith and Work Initiative, puts it this way: "We've reached a tipping point where the conventional wisdom that you keep your spiritual side at home is about to collapse."

Church and State

There used to be a commonly held belief that you could be anything you wanted to be in tech—except a Christian. Not so today.

A recent *Business Week* article reported that in 1986 only one conference on spirituality in the workplace could be identified. Today we have hundreds[14] of Work & Faith conferences, along with tens of thousands of workplace prayer groups and Bible Studies. In Silicon Valley alone, over 70 companies have said "yes" to faith diversity, including tech giants like Apple, Google, Facebook, LinkedIn, Salesforce, Dropbox, Cisco, and more.

---

13 https://www.shrm.org/hr-today/news/hr-magazine/pages/religion-at-work.aspx
14 http://www.intheworkplace.com/apps/articles/default.
asp?blogid=1935&view=post&articleid=68245&fldKeywords=&fldAuthor=Os%20Hillman&fldTopic=151

The vast majority of tech companies have come to the same conclusion, according to the annual Tannenbaum Report[15]: "If managed properly, sanctioning faith-based Employee Resource Groups can be an effective strategy for reducing religious bias and discrimination at work and improving talent attraction, retention and morale."

Many employees today are expecting to work at a company where they can talk as openly about their spirituality as they do any other part of their identity. It can be an immense relief to come out of hiding and share our true selves.

Gotta' Have Faith

Stepping into the B.S. on a daily basis takes endurance. Many times, we are struggling to change a world where systems are built to resist that change at all costs. A famous parable comes to mind.

Once a traveler came across an old woman who was stooped over what appeared to be thin sticks. He asked the woman what she was doing.

"I am planting orange trees," she explained.

The traveler thought this was a waste of her time.

"Why do you bother?" he asked. "You are an old woman. These saplings will take years before they will be old enough to bear fruit. You will be long gone by then."

"True enough," she answered. "I don't plant these trees for

---

15 https://tanenbaum.org/wp-content/uploads/2014/08/Tanenbaums-2014-Report-for-Corporate-Members.pdf

myself but for those who will come after me, just as those before me planted the trees that bear the fruit that I eat today."

Have faith in yourself and your ability to make an impact on a problem you want to solve today, this year, or in the next ten years. Speak up even if the idea sounds outlandish in your head, and understand how you can, care, and are ready to do. By trusting ourselves, we can effectively drive change to address the biggest, most contentious problems facing the world today. I know this (or this I know) because I have seen trust in action work on every level: within individuals, teams, and systems. Even this book you are reading was an act of trust; it came to be when I finally moved from can and care, to do—and so can you. I have faith!

12

Act Right Now

How do we fix the human built system (B.S.) so that we don't keep damaging the natural system and working against the issues we are trying to address today—especially when so many around us are dead set on upholding the status quo?

As a society, we are losing trust in these systems. Right now, we have the lowest level of trust in government and media and the highest trust in business at 61 percent. What's even more interesting for me is that the majority of employees, 77 percent, say that they trust their employer.

For employees—trust is paramount. Trust must be seen and felt. Trust in action is all about the bravery we embrace as we step into the B.S. and interact with the norms and rules surrounding how we should act and think.

The I in Team

Take for example my favorite corporate jargon phrase: There is no "I" in team.

Well, there is an I in team—if you are fearless enough to find it.

We smile when we hear this phrase because we know the truth. Literally, there is no 'i' in the spelling of team. But figuratively, we are conditioned to never overuse "I" when we are speaking—it seems too selfish and too self-promoting. In school, on the playing field, and in most settings, we are told that we must think of others first, which is foundational to trust and care.

However, part of caring is also speaking the truth and choosing conflict over conformity—preventing "groupthink" from happening. We must create a safe space to speak up if we see an opportunity to make things better. To do that, we need to find the I in team.

Trust Thyself

Trust in self is critical, especially in today's world.

I keep returning to the concept of Martec's Law. As I mentioned in Chapter One, Martec's Law states that technology is advancing faster than organizations can adapt, while individuals are adapting ahead of systems. Individuals have the advantage over both businesses and governments because we are quicker to adapt, and we can learn when not constricted.

One of the proofs of this is that we are living in an age of unprecedented global mass protests[16]. The scope, size, and frequency of the protests in this past decade alone overshadow historical eras of unrest such as the 1960s, 1980s, and early 1990s. Why are we seeing so many protests now? Because technology has empowered individuals. From Iranian citizens demanding freedom from an oppressive regime to the backlash against police brutality sparked in Minneapolis, when individuals have had enough, you see a protest. When leaders are willing to fight the fight, you see a whistleblower, and this past decade has brought us many, including Francis Haugen[17] bringing awareness to the harm Instagram does to young women or the many #MeToo survivors who came forward over the past decade to tell their stories and share their pain. People are trusting themselves more, and it's not just protesting against government—it's everything.

Rise of the Individual

Another story that dominated headlines recently was the 2022 FIFA World Cup.

FIFA World Cup proudly stated on its website: "FIFA is working with governments, local and regional development agencies, human rights groups, international and local

---

16 https://www.csis.org/analysis/age-mass-protests-understanding-escalating-global-trend

17 https://petapixel.com/2021/10/26/whistleblower-instagram-more-dangerous-than-other-social-media/

non-profit organizations, and former players to promote a fairer, more equal society through football."

The irony is that they are holding the World Cup, the world's largest sporting event, in Qatar this year. Qatar has a troubling human rights record and has come under scrutiny recently for its treatment of migrant workers and the criminalization of homosexuality. FIFA is more than capable, so why would they do this? We are certain they care, and yet, they still failed to *do* the right thing.

In response, during a press conference in Qatar, the president of FIFA told hundreds of reports "I'm European. For what we Europeans have been doing around the world in the last 3,000 years, we should be apologizing for the next 3,000 years before starting to give moral lessons to people."

He continued to highlight the commercial success of FIFA, which is a perfect example of an organization not getting the current times. Financial success may impress your investors, but it doesn't meet the requirements of so many other stakeholders. While we may be a ways off from the tipping point when the public turns off their TV sets and stops watching the games, individuals have taken up the mantle where organizations have failed.

An image of the Iranian national team made headlines because the players refused to sing their national anthem due to the ongoing human rights violations in their country, where 400 protestors have been killed and thousands arrested. As patriotic as I am, seeing them put their lives and livelihoods on the line because of the issues at home is a sign of leadership I highly respect.

The captain of the Iranian football team, Ehsan Hajsafi[18], said this to the press: "We have to accept that the conditions in our country are not right and our people are not happy. Before anything else, I would like to express my condolences to all of the bereaved families in Iran. They should know that we are with them, we support them, and we sympathize with them."

They should have been celebrating but instead they were using their platform to bring awareness to inequities faced by others back home and accepting the responsibility of whatever backlash may come. This is what it looks like when sports take a backseat to human rights and individuals use their platform as a stage to speak out and act. It puts trust into action because it shows others you care more about the topic than you do about your own well-being. This is the foundation of trust in action.

Another example from FIFA was the Japanese national team and spectators. The Japanese players left the locker room immaculate after the game, and photos of fans who stayed late to help clean up the stadium went viral on the internet. Everyone agreed that was a remarkable use of individual power on their part to show what goodness, kindness, and action does.

The point is, people are representing themselves in the most amazing ways. Systems may be full of controversy and failings, but there are ways for people to stand up.

---

18 https://conservativehome.com/2022/11/24/garvan-walshe-ehsan-hajsafi-irans-captain-is-the-true-hero-of-qatars-sordid-world-cup/

Up to Us

"We urgently need every business, investor, city, state and region to walk the talk on their net zero promises. We cannot afford slow movers, fake movers or any form of greenwashing."

—António Manuel de O., United Nations[19] Secretary General

The U.N.'s Integrity Matters report is undoubtedly a signpost for us: a call to arms for enterprise organizations to stop claiming that 'measuring' equates to 'taking action', and to governments around the world that legislation is urgently needed to make sure change happens.

A recent human rights assessment[20] that focused on 127 companies in several industries found that although there was some improvement, change has been slow. Despite the fact that updated methodology has raised the bar, only 66 percent of food and agriculture companies, 65 percent of ICT companies, and 57 percent of automotive companies had improved their scores on key human rights indicators since being included in the benchmark. Only 2 percent of those assess issues with suppliers and disclose progress.

It is startlingly clear that more needs to be done in order to ensure we don't exceed the 1.5°C warming limit set out in the Paris Agreement or miss our biodiversity goal before this decade is over. With every five weeks that pass, we edge 1 percent closer to the end of the 2020s—the most decisive decade

---

19 https://www.linkedin.com/company/united-nations/
20 https://www.worldbenchmarkingalliance.org/publication/chrb/

of our lives for the climate crisis and for the sustainability of our planet more broadly.

You've heard the phrase a watched pot never boils. Listening to the news feels a lot like watching the water boil. Doing is about action. We are watching the water boil in our oceans quite literally. We have more pledges, but less action. Companies are more transparent about their commitments, but the gap between promises and performance continues to worsen. At the end of the day, it's about changing behavior. We can keep blaming companies for the situation we find ourselves in, but who can change faster? Individuals.

So, what constricts us?

Well, for one, the white noise of built systems: the constant drone of negativity we see in our news and social media feeds every day. Also, ourselves. Our fears about not fitting in and our fears about failing. Yet for change to happen—based on Martec's Law—individuals need to take action. Because we adapt the fastest, the onus falls on us to ask ourselves the hard questions.

Do I trust myself? If we can't answer yes to this, then how can we play our role in our team?

Transforming systems starts with transforming ourselves. Each of us must believe we can make an impact and then act. So, yes, there is an 'I' in team; it's there if you're willing to find it. And I'm asking you to look for it because, if you do find it, it can change the world.

We need systems to exist and protect the vulnerable, but when the systems start to strain, it holds back change. When a built system is violating human rights or the natural system upon which we all rely, individuals can do something to prevent the 'train wreck' from happening. The key thing to remember here is that systems are built by humans for humans which means we can change the constraints at any time. Regardless of how broken our systems are, every day, we are a part of teams that are working to address the biggest challenges we face. In a world full of uncertainty, never forget you may be the one who has the ability to see the solution.

When sitting back and watching the water boil becomes too much, it's time to show others what it means to put their interests ahead of your own and be the one who embodies the adventure. Find trust in action by simply doing something.

The Day the World Stopped (and Restarted)

In February 2019, leading up to DAVOS, the world was setting the stage to address climate change. Ironically, mother nature chose that exact moment to put humanity on a time out. Amidst the chaos of COVID, we witnessed how quickly the natural system could recover from previous damage and effectively operate when mankind suddenly stopped polluting. During the lockdowns, there was no travel, no production, no commuters clogging up the freeways on their way to the office. You could see the monuments in India as the air quality improved for the first time in decades. There were clear skies over Los Angeles as the perpetual cloud of smog lifted. For all the bad and havoc COVID wreaked, we also saw what humans could do when they act.

The coronavirus pandemic was one of this generation's

scariest moments in addition to wreaking havoc on the world economy, causing more than 6 million deaths worldwide, and bringing the world to a standstill. By the same token, we also saw what could happen when we needed to come together as a global community to address a threat.

We saw systems working together for the first time. Government worked with regulators and individuals worked with businesses to find solutions at a record-breaking pace. Roadblocks were removed, companies focused resources and talent to resolve problems—and we did. It only required systems and teams to re-evaluate every aspect of work and collaboration to focus on the issue at hand.

The fact of the matter is we could do this across *all* the sustainable development goals if systems and teams would treat the various threats to our world the same as COVID-19. Many systems are in danger—food and water shortages among other things—and yet, instead of companies and governments collaborating, we are seeing the rise of protectionism, especially in developed countries. This is limiting our global ability to address inequalities throughout systems like education, standards of housing, health, food, and water scarcity. Without collaboration, we will not be able to address larger, immediate issues which will continue to chip away at society's trust in the B.S.

Hit it Out of the Park

As a change agent and action-oriented leader, it is easier to focus on what's broken in the system instead of acknowledging where things are working. It's like the old adage, "If all you have in your tool box is a hammer, everything looks like a nail." In this case, if trust is falling, trust must be missing everywhere.

While I use can, care, do to evaluate any situation or challenge I face, I also hold myself accountable. It is important to acknowledge when the system is actually operating beautifully. Sometimes the system can transform itself and you, as long as you are willing to plug in, see the connections, and accept that you can be changed by the system.

That's just what happened to me in December, 2021 on a dreaded trip to the Dominican Republic. My 12-year-old son Lawson had started a baseball charity to give children equal access to equipment, education, and food, and I was to be his proud chaperone on the inaugural trip. If it weren't for my child's passion for baseball and my goal to be a supportive dad, I would not have been in the Dominican Republic. One important fact—of the two Masseys in this story, one of us loves sports and the other doesn't.

I don't follow sports. In fact, I believe professional sports drive many of the built systems I most fiercely oppose, like income inequities, worker rights issues, gender inequities, and so on. My distaste for sports is enough that I would even say, prior to this trip, I didn't value professional athletes. But my son does love sports, and I recognized he was doing a good thing trying to change the system from within with the help of a mentor, a family friend who happened to be a first-round draft pick for the New York Yankees (someone I assumed was the exception to my norm). So, I put aside my resistance and agreed to accompany my son.

I went into this trip selfishly to help my son change a

"broken" system, and I quickly realized that the system was already on its way to making things more fair. It wasn't broken at all. So, this passive chaperone was in for a surprise.

At the kick-off dinner on our first night, I sat with some people among whom happened to be a pitcher for the Milwaukee Brewers, a shortstop for the St. Louis Cardinals, and a former outfielder for the New York Yankees. They told me how, in the weeks leading up to this trip, they were in their local communities planting trees with fans and their partner One Tree Planted (yes, the very same organization I partnered with to plant 50 million trees). The built systems I had an issue with were being challenged and changed from within by MLB—the same as my team had been with our environmental program.

We were sharing best practices, scale, impact—all the corporate buzzwords were happening at dinner, in a world I thought was nothing more than going to a game, having a hotdog, and doing the 7th inning stretch. Now I know it is so much more than that. We continue to partner with these leaders who use their platform to walk their talk.

With the help of these leaders, I was changed for good. And that's how I know a system can change an individual—though it's easily missed, if we aren't fearless enough to see it. I realized we were doing good stuff; I just had to open my eyes to it. We were doing it at work, at home, and now I could join efforts with professional athletes to do even more good with my son in the Dominican Republic and beyond.

I haven't always been fearless, and I know why—trust. Trust is the cornerstone to the built systems in which we operate. As the old saying goes: "A system is only as strong as its weakest link." To me, that means we must trust ourselves first as individuals if there is any hope of transforming teams and systems.

13

Ready. Set. Go.

Throughout my career, I have always known trust mattered. We are told constantly that trust is the foundation of all relationships. To me, it was very clear when trust was being eroded, but I also realized I didn't fully understand how to build trust, or in some cases, repair it. Like many things in our lives, trust is hard to define and measure, yet obvious when not there.

Of course, having a vague understanding of trust isn't enough if we truly believe this is the basis of relationships and everything we do as humans. We must be able to define, understand, and evaluate trust.

My hope is that this book has provided the tools so you can

quickly assess where and how trust is being broken and easily take actions that foster or rebuild that trust. Oftentimes, this takes the form of identifying a problem or an area where we want to make an impact, putting others' interests ahead of our own, and forming strong relationships to tackle the challenges we have ahead of us.

So, now that you are done reading the book (thank you) and you're ready to act right now, you might be asking yourself—what comes next?

When you put this book down, I'd like you to embrace every issue as an opportunity to step into the B.S. Whenever you find yourself within a system where you are unable to create the change you desire, remember the Trust Model. Identify which element is missing: can, care, or do. Then evaluate if trust is missing within self, team, or system. Within seconds, you can begin to identify new opportunities to continue to drive action toward your goal. I know this has served me through my career, and I hope it helps you make both the impact you want and the one the world needs.

I'd like to reiterate that we are in the decade of our lives. Every five weeks, we lose 1 percent of this critical decade. We are already more than 20 percent through with little progress made. It is clear, if we are going to make progress, we can't wait.

Remember who is responsible?

I am.

You are.

Our teams.

Our companies.

If you take one thing away from this book, I'd like it to be that trusting *yourself* will be a game changer. When we trust ourselves, we can take the action to transform our teams to transform our world.

There is no better feeling than to accept your own capability and take action to change something that isn't working. It is easy to let the white noise of the built system fool you into feeling insignificant or unable to make a difference. What we face can be daunting; knowing you have what it takes is enough to bend the curve on any topic covered throughout the book. Leveraging your trust in self to inspire those around you is how we change the system, piece by piece.

On that note, I'd like to leave you with a quote from climate-change activist Greta Thunberg from her speech at COP25 in 2019, when she astutely noted, "The biggest danger is not inaction. The real danger is when politicians and CEOs are making it look like real action is happening when, in fact, almost nothing is being done, apart from clever accounting and creative PR."

We must show that we are making meaningful progress towards our commitments. Without this, we just have nice propaganda. We must walk our talk. We don't have time. The environmental and human crisis is real and only we, the leaders, the individuals, can change the B.S. for the better.

We can do this. We are in this together.

Finally, I would love to hear from you if you have any ideas on how we can strengthen *Trust in Action*. If you'd like to contact me, you may do so at my website: www.jimmassey.co. If you would like to book me for a speaking engagement, contact Big Speak.

About *the* Author

Jim Massey is recognized as a global thought leader on trust, sustainability, and ethics. On the front lines of business transformation, he has led and developed groundbreaking programs ranging from Ambition Zero Carbon, one of the world's boldest corporate environmental programs, to launching the first Corporate Trust Report, laying out a blueprint for how businesses can build trust with a wide range of stakeholders.

Jim holds a Master of Science degree in Organizational Development from Johns Hopkins University and a Bachelor of Science degree in Business Administration from the University of Missouri. He is married to Emily and they enjoy the struggle of the juggle as they pursue their life's work and raise Sawyer and Lawson. The family loves the outdoors, travel, and finding their next adventure.

Made in the USA
Middletown, DE
10 April 2023